The Write Quotes - Book 1

From 500+ Author Interviews

INSPIRATIONAL & PRACTICAL
REFLECTIONS on

The Writing Life

Compiled by author and book podcaster
LANDIS WADE

Foreword by
Sarah Archer

The Write Quotes: The Writing Life

Book 1 in The Write Quotes series

Landis Wade

Foreword by Sarah Archer

ISBN print: 979-8-9876956-8-5

Library of Congress Control Number: 2023901583

The quotes in this book come from interviews and other publications on the Charlotte Readers Podcast audio podcast and website. The quotes have been edited for clarity and brevity.

Cover design: Dissect Designs

Book design: Jennipher Tripp

Publisher: Charlotte Readers Podcast, LLC
Charlotte, North Carolina

Printed in the United States of America

CONTENTS

Introduction - The Authors   7
Books in The Write Quotes Series   9
Foreword - Sarah Archer   11

THE WRITE QUOTES

The Writing Life   15

REFLECTIONS - LANDIS WADE

Lessons I Learned from the Quotes in
this Book   123
Why Start a Podcast and Publish this Series?   129

Acknowledgments   133
About the Podcast Hosts   134
Writer Index   137

INTRODUCTION - THE AUTHORS

From the fall of 2018 through January 31, 2023, Charlotte Readers Podcast published 324 regular episodes, 155 exclusive episodes, 28 video interviews, and 55 community blog posts. These 500+ interviews and blog posts feature authors in at least 33 states and five countries and serve as the source material for the eight books in *The Write Quotes* series. The range of publishing experience among the authors is vast, from authors published traditionally with large and small presses to hybrid and self-published authors. Some of these authors were happy to publish only one book, others are *New York Times* bestsellers with millions of books sold, and others are making their marks with readers one book after another.

This series is meant to inspire and educate by offering informative glimpses into the writing lives of published authors. Think of the quotes in these books as prompts for what works for you. Absorb what moves you and ignore the rest. At the very least, these quotes will give you a better understanding of how authors do what they do and how they feel about it.

The quotes in this series have been edited for clarity and brevity, and in order to reflect the spoken word nature of the interviews, the punctuation, grammar, and phrasing have not been perfected. All the authors in *The Write Quotes* series are listed in the Writer Index at the back of this book. Every author who appeared on the podcast or published a blog post on or before January 31, 2023 is quoted in at least one of the books in the series. Learn more about Charlotte Readers Podcast and sign up for the podcast newsletter to get access to interesting readerly and writerly content at www.charlottereaderspodcast.com.

Books in The Write Quotes Series

Learn how to order books in the series at
charlottereaderspodcast.com

———

Book 1 - *The Writing Life*
Book 2 - *Learning to Write*
Book 3 - *Writing Process & Tools*
Book 4 - *Storytelling, Inspiration, & Research*
Book 5 - *Writing Techniques & Characters*
Book 6 - *Writing Community, Revision, & Editors*
Book 7 - *The Emotional Writing Journey*
Book 8 - *Publishing and Book Marketing*

FOREWORD - SARAH ARCHER

One of the best parts about joining Charlotte Readers Podcast as a co-host has been expanding my writing community to include our listeners, contributors, and author guests. And one of the best things about the writing community is that it loves a lively debate. That spirit comes through in these pages. While many of the authors quoted here echo each other's perspectives, sometimes they conflict. Do you have to feel inspired to sit down and write? Is it ever too late to start a writing career? Do you find the drive to write within or because someone else encourages you?

Above the differences, one common theme that surfaces from these quotes is the *need* to write. The four-days-in-the-desert sort of thirst. Our authors express this idea in different ways. Some mention that they've wanted to write since they were children, or that it's all they ever wanted to do. They record the difficulties of writing—how time-consuming, unprofitable, mentally taxing, and emotionally demanding it can be—and then they say that they love it anyway. Some talk about characters inside their heads shouting to have their stories told, or claim that they feel driven to write to discover what's next in a story that's already inside them. Many say that they write because they can't *not* write.

Storytelling is an essential human need, probably as old as fire. And it's similar to lighting a match: creating energy out of darkness, conjuring something out of nothing. What we do as writers is mysterious, thrilling, ancient—and intimidating. Challenging. Sometimes maddening, or tedious. No matter how much you love your craft, you probably have moments when you want to throw out your computer or notebook and go work at a sloth sanctuary or something instead. Believe me, I've been there.

In those times, I hope you can turn to this book and sample some of its quotes for inspiration, a reality check, or just a reminder that you're not alone on this journey, and that what you write matters. People need stories. If you have a story that you feel the need to tell, I like to think that's because there's someone out there who needs to hear it.

THE WRITE QUOTES

The Writing Life

It's never too late to start writing.

— Maureen Ryan Griffin

In the best of times, nothing can compare, and in the worst of times, it's totally miserable.

— Craig Nova

The aspiration of every writer is a book that will pay their way into some good restaurants.

— Peter Reinhart

Most lawyers are not crazy about being lawyers. You spend your life in conflict and billing your time in six-minute increments. And then there's John freaking Grisham. He built this bonfire upon this mountain that says, look how great this life can be.

— JOHN HART

There's nothing I could have told myself that 21 years of writing novels haven't taught me. I've had to make so many mistakes. And I've had to make them over and over and over again to get to the point that I'm at now where I feel like I'm just in the zone.

— LISA JEWELL

One young guy went right to the chase immediately, he said, how much money did you make? And I said, about 12 cents an hour.

— ROBERT INMAN

Many of the things that I've written, people ask, how long did it take you to write that? I say, 30 years, and they say, wow, I guess I'm not gonna write.

— MARTIN SETTLE

You're born with that little voice in your head, that little voice that tells you to keep going. And it's the only thing that keeps you going. Because without that little voice, we quit.

— Steve Berry

I have the easy job. I just have to write the stories. Other people have the job to take what I've written and deliver it to the rest of the world. And that takes a lot of highly talented, highly specialized, highly motivated people.

— David Baldacci

The life that this affords is so unbelievably wonderful. I refer to it as the ultimate expression of personal freedom. You make enough money to do what you want, and you get to live where you want and write what you want. And I feel deep down that the universe must have plans to take that all away.

— John Hart

Writing is not about writing, necessarily. Writing is about living. And the more deeply and fully you live, the more you're able to write.

— ANTHONY ABBOTT

Write what you love. If what you know and what you love are the same thing, that's wonderful, but if not, pick the one you love. You're going to be much happier.

— STEVE BERRY

I know it sounds kind of cliché, but each book really is a journey. I never know where I'm going to end up and how I'm going to have changed by the end, not just my characters, but me and my thoughts and my opinions about things and my writing.

— JENNIFER MCMAHON

My agent said, and other authors have said it, it's a marathon, it's not a sprint. If your first book hits the *New York Times* bestseller list, more power to you, but I would say for 95% of us, that is not the case. And so you need to be ready for the marathon.

— ELLEN BUTLER

I think you want to have something that resonates enough with you that you're willing to spend a year or more writing about it.

— Maggie Smith

Writing shouldn't be a painful process that you find no joy in. Don't be your own critic.

— Martin Settle

If you're sitting in Hardee's and somebody in the next booth is having an argument, and you are a writer, you'll stay there and listen to the argument and see how it turns out. What you're listening to is the mechanisms of a relationship. And it's just all inspiring to know that there are these things called people, and they have relationships, and there's something going on between them. And you can observe that and play around with it as a writer. It's like being a crazy birdwatcher.

— Clyde Edgerton

There is nothing in my life other than the first time I held my two children in my hands that compares with holding a book in your hand, that's actually been published, that you wrote, with your name on the cover.

— MICHAEL ALMOND

You have to be the right temperament because you have to be alone a lot with yourself. So you have to be comfortable with that or you're going to find all kinds of excuses.

— MICHAEL POLELLE

I love going into the library and seeing how many people have checked my books out. It's just fun to see like, oh, my God, people are reading this thing.

— HOPE ANDERSON

Any writer can probably relate to that idea that it doesn't feel like there is a finish line, even when you finish the book.

— CAROLYN BAKER

I think if you love your work, and you want to share it, be professional about it, please. I am a believer in editors and proofreaders and beta readers, and hiring people who are creative in cover design, and I think it's worth the effort to treat your work just like a publisher would. And then go to town. Share it.

— HOLLY HUGHES

The writing is the fun part. Getting published is hard work.

— MURIEL SHEUBROOKS

When your first book comes out, you're all excited. You're like, ooh, I'm published, and it's coming out with either a small press or even a big publisher and you think, oh, everybody's gonna run out and buy my book. And the reality is, they don't. It's a long haul.

— ELLEN BUTLER

There's a lot of good histories out there and I admire those who do it. But if you can pack a bunch of true history into a great story, that's a fun challenge.

— SAM MCGEE

We're the only species that tells stories, so to be fully human, I think this is a way to do it. I think all of the arts are a way to be more fully human.

— George Hovis

I don't write about characters that don't interest me because life's too short.

— Mike Bond

When I'm writing, I don't care about anything. It's the book, right? And I'm totally into that. And when that's finished, I'm the business person.

— Rose Senehi

As I grew as a person and as I had challenges in life and had to deal with those challenges and learn from those challenges, the lessons that I was learning started to seep into my story.

— Brett Marie

The truth of the matter is that publishing is a business. And so when you publish your book, the minute you start sending your book out into the world, it's a product.

— CHARLES FIORE

Before my children were born, I had this very disciplined schedule, and I had this idea of how everything had to be for me to write. And then my daughter was born and I'm like, well, things have to change or I will not be able to do this and teach and be a part of the world. So rewind, rethink.

— JILL MCCORKLE

Today with the internet, and all that goes with it, people are just not as patient as they used to be. They'll see a novel that looks really thick and they'll just avoid it like the plague.

— NANCY STANCILL

A good method for being a writer in general is asking yourself, who are my readers? Who are the people that this book is written for? Just asking yourself that question lets you build out how to reach readers.

— JACQUI CASTLE

If you're famous, you can write about anything. You can write a cookbook, a memoir about your dog, it doesn't matter. It's going to sell. Publishers are about selling books.

— ROBERT FITZPATRICK

Even if it's a dog of a story, your query letter should be hot enough to make them want to read and determine for themselves that it's a dog of a story.

— JOHN GILSTRAP

I have never stepped away from my writing for any period of time, in 50 years.

— KEVIN McILVOY

If you don't put your soul into it, if you don't bleed for it, you're kidding yourself. You're not a writer. You're a dilettante.

— John Hart

Books are like children, they don't respect time. You want this to be published in May, and they're like, you never said which May.

— Julia Jordan-Zachery

For meeting agents, meeting audiences, to be able to say what's at stake shows you know not only what you've created, but that you are speaking to an audience that your work is going to land with.

— Katey Schultz

The word that I always associate with independent bookstores is discovery.

— Alex George

My favorite part of writing is when I find something that I've written that I didn't realize I'd written and it resonates with me, which I think, okay, that's gonna resonate with the reader. The least favorite part would be the minutiae.

— BRAD TAYLOR

If you want to be a writer, you have got to take a look at your schedule and say, okay, when can I fit it in? What can I eliminate? If you want to write, it's got to be a commitment.

— JOEL BURCAT

Even if you're traditionally published, you've got to figure out how to sell your own books. And that means, you've got to figure out what they're worth to you in order to do it. And that's where the math comes in. People get migraines and stomach aches when I start talking math.

— PAMELA FAGAN HUTCHINS

I went from literally answering the phones at Verizon Wireless to a year later having this book. I kind of got the golden ticket syndrome where I got to go in Willy Wonka's chocolate factory. It was bizarre.

— JASON MOTT

Whatever it is that you're doing, you need to be really intentional about it because every single thing that you're doing that takes you away from the page is something that's taking you away from the page. Everything has to be weighed really, really well. Is it worth it for you to do X when you could be writing? Those are questions that I have to ask myself all the time.

— KRISTY HARVEY

I don't think there's any other type of work where the results are so completely disconnected from what you put into it.

— REBECCA HODGE

My main thought initially was, how do I get published? That's what I wanted to do. My desire was to be published. And then I realized, no, your desire is not publication, your real desire is to write well, and communicate well. And when you get to that point, you can let your words go into the universe and see what they'll become.

— CHRIS FABRY

I don't think you can write about criminal justice or murder or mysteries or thrillers if you hadn't seen both sides of the fence. And I've seen both sides of the fence. I'm the only person who flew on Air Force One and Con Air in the same year.

— WEBB HUBBELL

A lot of people who aren't writers, they call writing a hobby. And it's so upsetting to writers, because writing is like a compulsion. There are days we don't want to do it. Or we say, I'm never doing this again. And you always come back to it.

— ALLIE COKER

Creativity really makes me feel alive. I'm happiest when I'm involved in creative pursuits, when I'm in that state of flow. It's almost like meditation.

— MIRINDA KOSSOFF

Fiction is my happy place, especially romance because it's going to end happily, it's going to end with two people who are in love, and who achieve what they want. And that's such a rarity in real life that I think that readers need it, and I need it. And cozy mystery is the same way, with the added dash of justice.

— TARA LUSH

It's a lot of work, I'm not gonna lie. So when I think about how I divide up my day, I spend the morning on the business of writing. And I spend the afternoon on the act of creating. And I keep those as separate as I can, because if I mix them too much, the creative side never gets its due.

— PAMELA FAGAN HUTCHINS

The hardest part for me is taking care of the rest of my life, because my desire is to sit and write. My ideal day is to spend it writing.

— Judy Goldman

I've found the writing kind of cleans me out. It is kind of a magical thing.

— Susan Proctor

Drilling down into the memories and talking with each other about them is more fun than you can stand.

— Bud Schill

You kind of have to have a sense of humor.

— JD DuPuy

I still keep a journal by my bedside.

— Gilda Syverson

Writing sort of saved me and I thought, well, how can I use it to help others?

— ROSIE MOLINARY

I was in my 50s before I really discovered what it was I was supposed to be doing.

— RANDELL JONES

Stephen King said you have to enjoy the whole process. The whole process can be quite scary sometimes.

— CATHY PICKENS

I use my books as a way to explore questions that I have about anything, from motherhood to love to sex to food.

— JESSICA PETERSON

Until you get in the game, you can't learn what the game is about.

— RICK PRYLL

The nice thing about fiction is I can make my characters younger, smarter and better-looking than me. And then when I will look in the mirror in the morning, I realize my life is quite diverged from my characters.

— MARK DE CASTRIQUE

I really think that some people romanticize writing to their detriment.

— KIM WRIGHT

I really like to socialize and interact with people who are interested in writing.

— DAVID RADAVICH

I really reached this point where I felt like I could be a writer, or I could be a New Yorker. And I couldn't be both.

— JEFF JACKSON

It's the reason people are compulsive gamblers. You have a little bit of success and you think it's going to happen again.

— DAVID POSTON

I can't help but write. It's just the way I process the world. I interpret everything through story. And I really do believe stories are the shortest distance to the human heart.

— MARYBETH WHALEN

That moment, when all is possible, and you have a bunch of good stuff, I love that moment, because it's a little bit like the tip off of a basketball game.

— SCOTT FOWLER

Having a day job will certainly set you back in terms of writing.

— MARTIN CLARK

I'm a Shakespeare professor, which means, among other things, that I don't depend on the sales of my book to pay my mortgage.

— A.J. HARTLEY

Writing that last word is such a great feeling.

— FRANK MORELLI

The second book was harder in the sense that I had a deadline.

— AMBER SMITH

I'm at my happiest when I'm writing and my thoughts come on paper.

— BARBARA JOHNSON

People say, oh, I don't like writing, but I like having written. I say, then you're in the wrong job. I never hear a physician say, I don't like treating patients, but I love having treated them. That's not a doctor I would go to.

— SCOTT HULER

There's a lot of memory in my novel. But there's a lot of imagination in there too. And that's what makes it fun, to get to write something like that.

— JON BUCHAN

I think Elvis's dad said something to him, like, you know, Elvis, you need to decide whether you're going to be an electrician or a guitar player.

— PHILLIP LEWIS

I used to think real writers wrote all day long. But what I realized is I can't write for more than two hours at a time.

— HEIDI BROWN

You're accessing something that is ineffable. I'm not saying it's spiritual, I'm just saying it's very old, and we don't have tools to measure it.

— Aaron Gwyn

I'm definitely living the writer life of the not so rich and famous, which I think probably most writers are.

— Amy Willoughby-Burle

While writing can be such an individual and sometimes lonely endeavor, living that writerly life and pursuing all these aspects of promotion and platform doesn't have to be a lonely experience.

— Bess Kercher

There is no competition out there. Everybody's gonna buy all of our books, plenty of time, plenty of money, plenty of space, it's all good.

— Claire Fullerton

People are so suspicious of writers who make up things, which is what fiction writers do, right?

— DALE NEAL

I try to approach the independent author life as I'm not in competition with anybody. We're all trying to get our writing out there. And all stories have something to say. And so to be supportive, by engaging with other writers and readers, it is definitely the best approach.

— DORI ANN DUPRE

The younger version of me thought success was one thing. After going through it, I know what success really is. Just acknowledge that you wrote a book. A lot of people never do that. So have fun with that.

— SETH ERVIN

The moment that writing starts to sound like bagging groceries, I'm out.

— A.J. HARTLEY

I loved the research part of it. I could sit at the library just transcribing information into a notebook about what I found.

— Ed Di Gangi

When people ask me, do you do it every day, I feel like they're asking me, do you brush your teeth every day? And they're like, every day? And I'm like, yeah, because it feels better to do it every day.

— Kim Wright

Be patient, trust yourself, enjoy the process. Because unless you're John Grisham, this isn't a great money-maker. This is something you do because you love it, because these characters call to you. So enjoy the process.

— Ellen Morris

Newsflash, the burden is always on the writer, not the reader.

— Susan Zurenda

Welcome to being another small business owner.

— JADE DEE

I often tell people, if you don't hear voices in your head, find another profession. You know, writers hear their characters in their heads, they hear them talk.

— CARRIE KNOWLES

I think every author who's published anything has the experience of having somebody come up to them at a party and say, I've got this great idea for a story, how about you write it and we'll split the profits?

— JEANNE ADAMS

I feel like when I left my job to write full time, I just imagined I would be writing all day and all night, I would just be pumping novels out. And the biggest challenge has been trying to set a schedule.

— AMBER SMITH

I've had people in therapy say my parents don't want me to be a starving artist and I say, great, don't be a starving artist, but you could be an artist, right?

— Amy Williams

I used to joke with my wife when I'd go out the door, saying, I'm off to commit an act of literature, to raise the stakes really high.

— Charles Israel

My goal was how do I outsource the things that are tricky and not in my wheelhouse, and make it beneficial for them so that I can continue to just write?

— Danielle Stewart

What's so amazing about writing is there's no time limit, there's no expiration date. We've got writers now who self-publish at 14 and 15. And then we have people who publish in their 70s and 80s.

— Michele Tracy Berger

I don't think that there ever is a point where fiction is completely done.

— EMILY CATANEO

My son had to write a six-word memoir, and I said, well, write six simple words, and then get a thesaurus and find ten words that mean the same thing as your six words. I promise you that you'll see six words that go together in the coolest, most unusual, unique way that you would never have come up with on your own had you not seen it on the page. He's like, Mom, don't try to make me a writer.

— TRACY CURTIS

Sometimes publishing goes well, sometimes it doesn't.

— TRACIE BARTON-BARRETT

You have to run your own race, stop comparing yourself to other writers. Just run your own race and realize that your writing is going to follow a path and just do the best that you can to follow that path.

— ELLEN BUTLER

Publication is great, but at the end of your life, whether you publish or not, if your writing life has given you friends, and community and satisfaction, then honestly, that's a more valuable thing than publication.

— Heather Newton

There's a lot of solitude to writing. It's rewarding in a way that's kind of hard to describe.

— Mary Tribble

Books take over your life. Once the story is there, that's all you think about. And it can be really overwhelming. I learned I had to shove that out, focus on the sentence in front of me, the paragraph in front of me, the page in front of me, and just write.

— Emme Lund

Being a writer, impostor syndrome is a really heavy burden. I'm not over the imposter syndrome for being a lawyer.

— David Rudolf

When people say, well, I might like to be a writer, we talk about the craft of it, and sitting your butt in the chair and doing it, but also finding a community.

— MAGGIE SMITH

A number of times I've said that I'm done. I'm not playing this game anymore. That generally will last for a few months. And then I'll have an idea for a book and it needs to get written somehow.

— A.J. HARTLEY

Be patient. But at the same time, be confident in your own voice. Don't try to structure your book by what's currently popular in the market, or add elements to it that you think will have appeal simply to add them rather than be authentic. And learn the business of publishing.

— C.J. BOX

Most writers have a day job. If you can focus completely 100% on writing, how lovely for you. I think that there are very few writers who can sustain themselves just on writing.

— Robert Gwaltney

My idea of hell is being stuck somewhere without a book.

— Craig Johnson

You put a little piece of yourself, sometimes more, in each book.

— Donna Everhart

I have a hard time calling myself an author. The technical words are, I have authored two books.

— Fabi Preslar

My poetry is very intentionally grounded in my experiences, my identity as a woman of color, who grew up in the rural South, who lives in the South, who has experienced all the good, bad, ugly joy of the South, and helping people find themselves inside of that conversation, and other kinds of conversations about what it means to be human.

— Jaki Shelton Green

Every day, I'm doing something related to my writing career.

— Jenifer Ruff

I control my own schedule. I work from home. I can stop and take a break in the middle of the day to walk the dogs if I need to think something through, which I could never do when I worked in an office job. They didn't like you to wander around thinking.

— Jodi Helmer

The best advice I've ever gotten and the advice I always give is write the next book. This has been very important to my path. It is always about that next book in the series.

— Danielle Stewart

When writing is going well and I'm into a story, it is a great opportunity for me to spend 90 minutes a day doing something that I love and creating and exercising those muscles. When the story isn't going so well or when one piece won't come together, man is that tough.

— J.A. Walsh

I could be living anywhere and have things to write about, because I think one of the keys to being an essayist is to be an observant human being.

— Patrice Gopo

Writing made my life richer because anytime you can tap into your creative subconscious, it adds something to your life.

— Sandy Hill

Characters are always foremost to me. All of my books
have inciting incidents, but the books are not about the
inciting incidents. The books are about the relationships
between the characters.

— WILEY CASH

Teaching creative writing fulfills me. I'm not going to
make a living off my books, most likely, and so it's the best
quality of life to have a day job that instead of taking away
from my writing, it enhances it.

— CALEB JOHNSON

It's interesting because what we're talking about is doing
something that you love that might never garner a living
wage for you.

— CAT WARREN

The writer Larry Brown said, remember, no matter how many books you sell, no matter how successful you are, it always comes down to you in a room doing the work. It wasn't that I didn't know that necessarily, but there was something about the way he said it, and maybe the setting and the time, that it really struck.

— MICHAEL CROLEY

The sooner you start writing, the better.

— TOM HANCHETT

It's sort of like the dream scenario for a writer to have your first novel actually sell and sell to a major publisher.

— SARAH ARCHER

Writing is just a gift, whether it turns into a story that gets published or shared with people or it's just for our own edification. It's a fabulous process.

— AMY WILLIAMS

James Dickey had some of the most wonderful quotes and I'd love to tell you one thing he said. He said, there's a difference in writers. You can watch people playing tennis. Some tennis players are out there to win. Others are out there not to lose. And he said it's the writers who are out there to win who are going to make it.

— DANNYE ROMINE POWELL

Every time I sit down to write a book, it's as if you've never written a word in your life.

— DAVID JOY

There's no wrong way to write. You just need to decide for yourself what you want out of your writing. If you don't care about ever making money off it, that's perfectly okay, you're still a writer.

— GAIL MARTIN

I don't know a good writer who's not a voracious reader.

— RON RASH

There's a lot of waiting in writing. For me, the best way of dealing with that is to be working on something new, whether it's a novel or a short story.

— Heather Bell Adams

It's a fun job. I am thankful I get to do it because I can imagine anything, I can write about anything, and I can be anywhere. I tell people all the time that if they have any interest in doing it to jump in. Everyone has a story to tell.

— Joy Callaway

I can bring in a bunch of writers who say that writing is hell.

— Lee Matalone

An ideal world would be to wake up, have coffee, do a little exercise, and then sit down in my study at my desk and write. That's the ideal world.

— Mary Bess Dunn

If no one has just gifted you with a bag with a million dollars in it to live off of, you have to have a job to pay your rent while you're trying to pursue your creative goals. Also, no feeling of success lasts forever.

— MARY LAURA PHILPOTT

I have since been schooled and been told, no, Molly, you are an author, you have written books. It was a mental challenge and easy to sort of self-deprecate over that and just sort of brush it off. At least it was for me.

— MOLLY GRANTHAM

If you want to be a writer, you can't just wait for the inspiration to hit like in a movie where you stay up all night and then you finish your great American novel. That does not work. You have to put in the hours. You have to have a schedule. You have to treat it like a job.

— NATASHA TYNES

I would be very content with a dedicated core of readers that really appreciated the work and really appreciated the stories.

— REITA PENDRY

If someone were to say, hey, we need you to spend eight
hours a day, seven days a week doing nothing but writing,
on the one hand, sure, that'd be a dream, but you know,
an impossibility.

— AMY WILLOUGHBY-BURLE

The highs can be really high, and the lows can be really
low. But if you're able to sort of absorb feedback, and
allow yourself the space, just sort of marinate in it a little
bit, what I found is you can definitely learn and grow and
improve.

— BESS KERCHER

The creation of art is a depiction of what it means to be
alive.

— CLAIRE FULLERTON

I always get up in the morning thinking this could all be taken away from me so I better hustle today, and that's what I've done. I've just kind of worked at my own pace, which is a lot faster than a lot of people. I'm able to juggle many different projects in the same day.

— M. WILLIAM PHELPS

My parents said, well, what about your aspirations to be a writer? And I said, I'm letting it go. I don't know if it'll ever come back, I'm just gonna have to abandon myself to divine providence and see where it leads me. Twenty years later, I got my book, and the writing came back.

— PETER REINHART

It felt good to write that thing and be done and finish it. I mean, honestly, we had so much in the air, it was like, how do we land the plane? I'm really glad we landed the plane.

— SETH ERVIN

I would tell my younger writing self that it's not going to be perfect. You can sit here from now until the coming of the apocalypse and it's not going to be perfect. No book is perfect. No story is perfect. You just have to serve the story, serve your characters, and give the reader an experience.

— Tracy Clark

I always thought writing was a way to make money for myself. But it turns out that it's an emotional outlet as well. I'm very happy to know that when things happen that are difficult, I do try to take time to put pen to paper.

— Wilnona Marie

The only advice that I would give my younger self would be to enjoy it, and to relish every moment that I had to create and also relish every moment that I had to be out living and amassing the experiences that would go into this story.

— Brett Marie

I would tell my younger self to try to relax and enjoy the ride. Don't put so much pressure on yourself. I'm giving myself that advice right now, at this present stage. So let's hope I can take it now.

— CHRISTY HALLBERG

I should not have wanted so much to be a writer. I should have wanted more to write.

— ED SOUTHERN

Don't expect it to get any easier. It's not very encouraging advice.

— FRYE GAILLARD

You can't rush any of this. In fact, I think that is a problem with some writers when they're new to it.

— IRENE BLAIR HONEYCUTT

It's interesting, as writers, there's this tension between this work that is so solitary, and yet, it is so social. When we send it out into the world, we want other people to read it. And we ultimately need other people to respond to it.

— JOANI ELLIOTT

You're always trying to think of the next character or where the story is supposed to go and I come to the desk every day, so yeah, it's all-consuming.

— PAUL ATTAWAY

It's almost this weird combination of a sense of urgency and patience that you have to put together and I'm a lot better at the sense of urgency than I am the patience.

— SAM MCGEE

It's an endless process of learning, and learning, and learning, and learning.

— WALTER BENNETT

As novelists, we're like magpies forever flying around looking for bright, shiny objects to pick up and put in our stories.

— ALEX GEORGE

I think there is a sense of calling in a writer's life that you can step into.

— CHRIS FABRY

There's a funny anecdote about Chekhov, where somebody said to him, this too shall pass, and Chekhov said, nothing passes. I think that that's true of writers.

— ERIC DEZENHALL

I left a paycheck in 1986 and ever since I've been doing what I call taking in laundry. I do what I can with the talents that I have available. I've been lucky and been able to find projects that were not only interesting but with which I can make a little money.

— HOWARD COVINGTON

One of my most frustrating points of being an author is that when you are an author of color, or a female author, or any kind of minority author, you're not allowed to just be the author. Wherever you go to an interview, they have to ask you, what's it like being a black author?

— JASON MOTT

I would have told my younger self that when you really wanted to write, you should have just made the time. The other thing I would tell the lawyer part of me is to relax a little bit more and not to be as tightly wound as I was. I tell the writer side of me to just enjoy myself and just go with it.

— JOEL BURCAT

The days of an author churning out a book and handing it off to Max Perkins, who then makes it take off, those days are over.

— JOHN GILSTRAP

Art is one way in which we express and absorb beauty. And without beauty, would we even be human? Would we even have society? I don't know that we could.

— KATEY SCHULTZ

I try always to understand, with clarity, with humility, that what I write is not for everyone, that it will be more powerful for some readers than others.

— KEVIN MCILVOY

I would tell my younger writer self to live hard, live fully, gather experiences, gather characters, and take better notes of all of it.

— PAMELA FAGAN HUTCHINS

I never thought of myself as a writer. And then about 10 years ago, I realized, oh my goodness, I have been writing my whole life.

— JANET SARJEANT

I would tell my younger writer self to trust yourself with the guardrails down, because as a lawyer, I realized in many ways my thinking was kind of rigid, at least for a novelist.

— MICHAEL POLELLE

For me, the most pleasurable and most rewarding aspect of making novels is the actual writing, it's that lonely long distance running of sitting in front of the laptop and living with those characters and recording their adventures and their discoveries and their trials and tribulations. To me, that is as lovely as this conversation.

— TERRY ROBERTS

I wrote in the acknowledgments that if you are one of those people who insists all novels are autobiographical, please skip chapters 9, 14 and 18. Also skip these chapters if you are my mother.

— KIMMERY MARTIN

I like the idea that my story can be helpful, that in a world that is stressful and chaotic, my words could bring laughter or inspiration or provoke thought, or at the very least, just provide enough of a diversion to ease the weight of the world. That is just dope to me.

— JAY WARD

I almost always learn something or realize something I didn't know before I started the work. The writing takes me deeper into my own experience and the deeper I go into my experience, the deeper I go into the collective experience of all human beings.

— KATHIE COLLINS

I really have kind of given up on the perfect balance. Everything sort of ebbs and flows. And as long as everyone's happy and everything's getting done, we're doing okay.

— KRISTY HARVEY

Part of the joy and beauty of writing is the unending possibilities of the blank page.

— SARAH ARCHER

The experience of hearing my father read stories to us is what made me into an English professor. It gave me a love of literature.

— MARK WEST

I used to have to actually mail my manuscript off to my editor in New York in a box. Yeah, I'm old. So when you think about the things you have to learn, you also have to think about the acceleration and change.

— CATHY PICKENS

Your writing is meaningful: to you and to your readers. You are never a fraud for putting a part of yourself out there. You are really rather brave.

— LUCY MCLAREN

Your books will outlive you. Remember this.

— D.S. DAVIS

It's magic. It's inspiration. I don't know what it is. It's just there and you, you capture it.

— RICK BLEIWEISS

My characters are never wholly me. But I'm sure there's always a piece of me in there as well.

— JON BASSOFF

I always have a book in process. When I finish one, I already have the ideas for the next one fleshed out so that I never have a space where there's nothing going on.

— JENIFER RUFF

My favorite thing about writing thrillers is also my favorite thing about reading them. I love putting together the puzzle pieces and trying to solve the mystery, not just of the plot, but the mysteries that are inside each of the characters as well.

— MEGAN MIRANDA

A lot of writing is just bricklaying.

— THERESE ANNE FOWLER

I would tell my younger writing self that writing is a business, and take business classes. I wish I could have seen the future, that I would be running my own small writing business one day. I would have been better prepared.

— BOBBY NASH

I think it's good to know that you can always sort of pivot, change your direction, even if it's only slightly or greatly, at any point in your life.

— BOBBY FINGER

In some ways, the topics of your fiction inform your brand, because you come to be known for the type of stories that you're writing.

— BECKY ROBINSON

I was talking to a friend who's also a novelist, Elizabeth Kostova, who's a very gifted novelist, and she said all novelists have bisexual imaginations. And I said I'm gonna quote you on that and she said, go right ahead.

— Terry Roberts

One of the things I hate in the children's literature world is this idea that kids are stupid, that you have to explain everything to kids, or that kids are somehow not as sharp as adults. No, it's actually the opposite. Kids are smarter than we are.

— Mark West

I had to know the rules before I could break them.

— Misha Lazzara

I'm lucky enough to be a full time writer, which is amazing. And when I feel like I'm being a hermit, and I haven't seen other humans for too long, I'll take my laptop and go in the cafe, and treat myself to a nice coffee. That's like the highlight of my week.

— Sophie Cousens

Just because I've written all these books doesn't mean that I'm ever going to master this craft of writing. I still make mistakes, I go down the wrong path. Sometimes I make a U turn. You just work through it.

— David Baldacci

The words will not write themselves.

— Paul Reali

Keep whatever it is that's driving you to write in mind and let that lead to your persistence.

— Culley Holderfield

I'm a very disciplined writer. I am writing two books a year right now for HarperCollins, a Christmas novel and a summer novel. I start very early in the morning in my robe about 6am with a lot of coffee before the world intrudes and I write for about five or six hours when everything is fresh. I just go until I cry, weep, laugh, stop.

— Wade Rouse

Writing for me is maybe a third or fourth chapter in my life.

— Kathy Izard

The guiding light has to be exactly what you just said, are you going to bore the reader?

— Nora Gaskin

I still remember my mother telling me, well, you would be good at that, you could do that, too, but you really need to find a way to support yourself. It was good advice for an 11-year-old.

— Cathy Pickens

The parts that surprise me are why I do this.

— Marybeth Whalen

I thought it would be easy to make money as a writer. It is definitely not. When I came to terms with that, I realized that the writing was the important part. I wish I knew that when I was 20.

— FRANK MORELLI

Just write the thing you want to write.

— LISA JEWELL

For me, each novel is different. Each novel is a new question. Each novel is a new adventure. And for me, that's vital, in the sense that it lives and breathes and bleeds. And it keeps me engaged at a level that I would never be engaged otherwise.

— TERRY ROBERTS

Writing any book, and particularly a memoir, is a matter of discovery. And I think it's that continual and surprising sense of understanding that changes you. And so the benefit of writing a book is what you learn about yourself, and what you learn about your material.

— CRAIG NOVA

In broadcast journalism, everything's got to be tight, buttoned up, minute 20, minute 30. And then you go a minute 35 and some producer says it's got to be a minute 30. Nobody tells you to do that in a novel. When I started writing fiction, it was so freeing because you can just ramble on as long as you want to ramble on.

— CLIFF YEARGIN

I think the way that we get past intolerance and towards acceptance and love is by knowing people in our lives who are queer, who are open about it, who are trans, finding out that they are regular loving people. And so I think one of the ways that we can do that and reach people widely is with something like a book or a story, something that lets us empathize with those characters.

— EMME LUND

Be honest with yourself. How far do you want to go with this book thing? Do you want to do it for the rest of your life? Is this a side gig? Is it just you want to write books, tell stories and have fun? If you really love to write and publish then do that, build your brand, promote yourself and your book, but if you want to publish once as a life goal and knock it off your bucket list, do that.

— STACY HAWKS

It used to be in the old golden days–I grew up on Hemingway–if you were an author, you could become a celebrity, right? Now you have to be a celebrity before you become a well-known author.

— MICHAEL POLELLE

I almost think of writing as like a life preserver for me.

— PAUL ATTAWAY

There's so many more ways to make money. Yeah. I quit all the others to do this one.

— CATHY PICKENS

It always felt good to be writing and to be out there connecting with writer friends and also just observing life and thinking, well, I could put that in a story, I could make a story out of that. And I'm always thinking that way, I'm always in the game.

— BRETT MARIE

I would say my personal moments as a writer are those moments when all of a sudden I see where it clicks together.

— JILL MCCORKLE

I've been a big believer in continuing to educate yourself, and stay abreast of what's going on all my life. And writing a book was just an extension of that basic process.

— GENE HOOTS

One of the reasons that I love the novel as an art form is that once you pit yourself against the novel, you're pitting yourself against paradox, which is, for example, can you come to terms with how a person can be two opposite things at the same time? Is it possible for a person to be absolutely a hateful racist of the most extreme kind, and be a person who is loving to the highest degree of their own grandchildren, their own community?

— KEVIN McILVOY

My biggest joy is to be done. Every time I write something and it's done, I swear, I'm like, I'm never gonna do this again.

— JULIA JORDAN-ZACHERY

I always thought to myself that sooner or later, I'm going to write a book.

— BRAD TAYLOR

For some people, that validation of a traditionally published deal is the end all and be all and more power to them. But for me, it was about not having to deal with everybody else telling me what to do.

— PAMELA FAGAN HUTCHINS

The reason why I write is because it's a world that I can control.

— ERIC DEZENHALL

I like to write not because I have answers about things, but because I have questions.

— AMBER SMITH

Why do I write? I can't not.

— CHRIS FABRY

I don't remember ever truly wanting to be anything else. It's been with me the whole time. I was always a writer.

— ALLIE COKER

I worked for a great editor at the *Atlanta Constitution* who said that journalism was the closest he would ever come to a religion.

— BOB DEANS

A large part of why I write fiction is because of the fun factor. It's a fun mental thing to do.

— TARA LUSH

My goal was to get published by a reputable publisher, and just to have the book, even just for my friends and family, so I could shut up all the doubters because everybody says you can't do it.

— JOHN HART

I have been writing primarily lesbian material. When I try to write something different, it doesn't feel authentic to me. It doesn't feel as meaningful.

— PAULA MARTINAC

As we grew up, we reminded each other the stupid stuff we did when we were kids, and one day, the three wives were all together, and they said, we think you should write these stories down. And we commenced to doing that. And for the next couple of years, we wrote this book.

— Bud Schill

I have wanted to be a writer since I learned how to form letters when I was five.

— Abigail DeWitt

I shouldn't complain about being a lawyer, but I do anyway, as most lawyers do. But, you know, I wouldn't have written this book about lawyers if I hadn't gone to law school.

— J.D. DuPuy

I had relied on writing growing up as a really good tool to process what I was going through.

— Rosie Molinary

The moment in the writing process that gives me special joy is usually when a scene works that you didn't think was going to work.

— MARK DE CASTRIQUE

She said, I'm not going to name the student here, I'm just going to read what the student wrote. And she read my story to the whole class. I was a shy child, and I was probably turning red, but at the same time, I was feeling for the very first time the power of story. And that was it. There. Yes, thank you, Mrs. Ballard.

— KATHRYN SCHWILLE

One of the reasons that we love to write is because we go to this magical place where we do forget ourselves. And if you're worrying about yourself and how good you are, you're not going to find that magical sweet spot.

— MAUREEN RYAN GRIFFIN

I write about the things that are important to me, and more importantly, I write about topics where individuals might have an opportunity to see themselves where they didn't always see themselves. That's my commitment as a writer that brings me back even when I get frustrated.

— Julia Jordan-Zachery

As soon as I learned how to write words, I had a notebook and a pen with me at all times. Harriet the Spy was my hero because it was somebody like me. She carried that notebook with her everywhere. And when I read that book, as a kid, I was like, oh, there are people like me out there.

— Marybeth Whalen

I write because I like it.

— Martin Clark

I love planning out a story and putting together a massive outline of all the little events that are going to happen and then before actually having written it, just being able to sit there and hold that in my hand and know that this is an idea that I'm going to bring to life.

— FRANK MORELLI

I've always wanted to write since I was about 14 years of age. I used to write little short stories, and I would hide them under my bed. My mom would find them and read them. And one day I caught her. And she was so interested. And from that day on, I just loved to write.

— BARBARA JOHNSON

I can remember wanting to be a writer at age four. I remember going out behind the house and scribbling little things down, and it wasn't until I started doing the job of writing that I found out what a joy it was to have people trust you with their stories, and share those stories. That's an incredible, incredible thing.

— SCOTT HULER

I thought about some of the experiences and cultures that had shaped me and I realized that not any one of them was particularly unique, but the combination of them was a little different. And so I thought I'd try to pull together some of those and see if I could make a story about it that also included some themes that were important to me.

— Jon Buchan

People deal with tragedy differently. For me writing this book was cathartic. It was therapeutic because I got to relive all of these experiences with Taylor that are gone now.

— Laura King Edwards

I love the routine of being a writer and I like the structure.

— Heidi Brown

It's always nice to see your book reach its readers.

— Belle Boggs

There's that old Flannery O'Connor quip that she writes because she's good at it.

— Jon Sealy

What is magical about it is you seem to be discovering it, just like a reader would be discovering it and encountering it for the first time. I used to not talk like this. But those are the things I love and that's why I write, to discover those things.

— Aaron Gwyn

I've met writers who think of the day to day writing as this incredible chore, this sort of miserable experience in order to get to the end of the book and hopefully a paycheck. Why do that? I don't. I like writing sentences.

— A.J. Hartley

I remember my seventh grade teacher who read something I wrote and said, you really didn't write this did you? And I said, why are you saying that? She said, because it's too good. And yeah, she was my inspiration.

— Edward Di Gangi

I write because I feel unbalanced if I don't write. I write to try to make sense of the world. I write to try to figure things out. I write to entertain myself. I write because I can't not write.

— MAUREEN SHERBONDY

I tend to write about things I need to work out, or work on myself in my own personal life. And I've always thought of writing as a kind of therapy.

— AMBER SMITH

The purpose of living a creative life is to have fun and to enjoy life and to be light-hearted and to be fully expressive.

— AMY WILLIAMS

So many people ask me, is it cathartic to write memoir?
And my answer always is no. That's what you write in a
journal. That's why you keep a diary. But when you write
memoir, you're really looking for self-understanding.
You're really looking to know yourself better. The reward
for writing memoir is self-understanding.

— Judy Goldman

I love starting a book that I do not know how it ends, and
I write it to find out what happens the same way I would
read a book to find out what happens. That's the most
fun part for me.

— Nora Gaskin

You are a writer before you're ever published. You are a
writer, because you are creative. You're on this earth, and
you love language, right? So before anyone validates you,
you are that.

— Michele Tracy Berger

Most of us get into writing because we're trying to
discover something about ourselves.

— Randell Jones

Your friends say, oh, you're going to try and write the great American novel, and you say, sure, that's what I'm gonna do, I'm gonna write a great American novel. And I came to realize, looking at the definition, I might not want to write a great American novel.

— RICK PRYLL

Bill Buckley was once asked whether he enjoyed writing and his response was I enjoy having written. I very much relate to that now, but I can say as well, as difficult as the writing was at times, it was a real joy to be digging into this historical record.

— ROBERT CONRAD

There are people who want to be writers, but they need a way to make a living. I was writing before law school and got back to it as soon as I could after law school. I've never wanted to write about lawyers or the law. I've always had the writer side of me instead.

— HEATHER NEWTON

It's always been kind of a dream of mine to write a book.

— Barry Swanson

Once you've written a book, it's kind of like that well is untapped and you realize, this can be done. I've thoroughly enjoyed the process.

— Robert Whitlow

What prompted me to want to write this book and begin this journey is I feel that I have an obligation to educate people. And the book is very educational.

— Roland Beckerman

I realized I did not want these stories to die in my head.

— Larry Farber

I would love to write another book. I had so much fun writing this one.

— Jennifer Dasal

I couldn't see how we co-author a book, so Brian, with his psychology background, manipulated me, saying, let's write five chapters and if it's working, we'll keep going, and if not, you can have the story. It was so fun to write with someone who's a good friend, we just never looked back.

— Jeffrey Wilson

If you're writing and you're counting the words, you're kind of missing the point. It's kind of like going on a trip and not looking out the window but staring at the odometer's little numbers as they click by. That's just not my idea of a good time.

— Craig Johnson

I had always wanted to write books ever since I was a kid.

— Anissa Gray

It opened up a whole new world for me. To all of a sudden have a career in your 70s is just ridiculous. It is so much fun.

— Mary Ann Claud

Writing has always been a release and a healing process.

— Rosy Crumpton

My poetry has always been something that helps me get through things.

— Kamaria Delaney

I like to get into something, write it and then get out. And you don't do that with a book. You're in it for a really long time.

— Jodi Helmer

There's a sense of calm and fun and love that I feel when I'm able to create. It makes me happy.

— Terra Kelly

I like to write things where there is the ability to imagine
that all of this could in fact happen.

— RITA WOODS

I write because I love having a platform to use my voice.
We live in a world where so many things are happening.
And some of us feel like we can't do anything. Some of us
feel like things we do don't make a difference. And I feel
like my books might make a difference. Even if it's
allowing somebody to escape for a couple of hours.

— SOPHIA HENRY

With a book, I felt like I could take what I was talking
about and reach more people.

— STACEY SIMMS

Going to the MFA program was a good thing for me. I did it much later in life. And that's one regret. But it taught me how to critique and how to read and how to do things I didn't particularly want to do like annotations. But it's part of being a good writer.

— Tamra Wilson

It meant everything the day that I received my first copy of my book that I got to hold in my hand. It was pretty emotional. It meant the world to me.

— Alison Klakowicz

I felt that my book was something that needed to be out there and that other individuals would benefit from.

— Betsy Mack

Every time I glance down at my cover or see my book in a store, I do a double take, because I come from a really rural blue collar place. I know a lot of storytellers. But I didn't know writers.

— Caleb Johnson

I write because it's my lane. It's where I have found extra value in myself.

— Danielle Stewart

The writing was really for me. And then I gave that writing to the public, especially to women or families dealing with breast cancer, to say, here's what I felt, to understand your own feelings if you're going through this.

— Donna Love Wallace

I'm having a blast with it. It's so much fun.

— John Gerdy

When I told my husband, I think I'm gonna write a book, I don't want to say that he didn't believe me, but he was like, sure, do whatever you want.

— Lexi Aidyn

It's shocking to me how many people are writing to survive, to create some sort of connection to feel like they're not alone.

— MEAGAN LUCAS

You have to do the best you can do to love the creative process and the art and try to put the business stuff out of your mind until it's time to put it in your mind, really.

— MICHAEL CROLEY

There's no better feeling in the world than to have someone read something that I've written and tell me that it made them think about themselves differently.

— NICOLE AYERS

It's still very surreal to me that I wrote this and that my story is out there for people to read and relate to.

— RACHAEL BROOKS

I really enjoy sitting down at my laptop and getting after it. It's a breath of fresh air. I've loved practicing law for all these years and had a lot of fun with it and had a lot of success, but it's nice to do something else.

— Vernon Glenn

When I'm writing, it's really cathartic. I get all of these–I hate this term–but aha moments, and there were so many of them.

— Camille Martin

I always wanted to write a book. From research to writing to now publishing, it took over two and a half years, so it's definitely been a long process, but I wanted to take my time to make sure that I got it right.

— Colin Cerniglia

I was reading an essay by poet Louise Glück the other day and she said, what poets miss when they're not writing is that deep concentration that you feel when you're trying to make a poem work. That's what we hanker after, not publication, not praise, not getting a book out, we long for that time when we're back into that deep concentration, because it blocks out everything else. And it's just so pleasurable.

— Dannye Romine Powell

Ron Rash was the first person to ever hand me a book that I absolutely fell in love with. I didn't even know that you could do what this book did. And the minute I read it, it was like, that's what I want to do. Because you're writing about my people. You're writing about my places.

— David Joy

My favorite writer is John Grisham and to paraphrase him extremely roughly, he said, in effect, he writes for entertainment. I was hoping people who read my books will just enjoy reading them.

— George Arnold

I enjoy seeing people have a good time, and being able to relax, forget about whatever problems are going on in their lives and just chill out for a couple of hours. And it's my hope that this kind of story does that for people.

— Ian Malone

I would like to go back and remind my younger self to step back a little bit, simmer down a little bit, and just have fun with it. And remember the joy that brought you to the project in the first place.

— Heather Bell Adams

It's a creative process. It's fun. It's a heck of a lot more peaceful than what I do 60 hours a week as a lawyer.

— Sam McGee

Writing books is the only thing I've ever really wanted to do.

— John Russell

Deep down, I have always wanted to write a novel.

— Jordan O'Donnell

Honest answer is one of the reasons I write is because it makes me less miserable.

— Joseph Mills

I had no idea it would get published or what would happen to it, but this was something on my little bucket list. If I just ended up stapling it together, this was something I wanted to accomplish. And then I did it, and my kids are very proud and my friends are like, this is amazing, you actually got this done.

— Katherine Snow Smith

I write because it gives me joy.

— Joy Callaway

Creativity continually is a source of inspiration, comfort, and solace in the world that we're in.

— Karen McElmurray

I had just gotten my contract, and I remember the first thing my mother said was, it honors her papa. And I was honoring her too. And then she said to me, she said for the first time, I know why I survived. And she said, I couldn't tell my story, but you can do it for me.

— Kathleen Burkinshaw

The whole thing is really about just writing and being with your words, and your computer, or whatever you write on. It's really not about all the other stuff about publishing and events and all of that other noise.

— Lee Matalone

Some people just like getting in a truck and driving with the windows down on country roads. I like to write and I don't always think what I write is good. I don't always want people to see it. I have plenty of things that never go anywhere. Endless documents that are half-written stories that end up nowhere. But for me, it just kind of helps me stay sane.

— MOLLY GRANTHAM

When the first book actually gets into your hands, you look at it, and you say, did I really write this? Did I really do this? When you have a hardcover book, in your hand, you are leaving something behind.

— PALOMA CAPANNA

I've tried not to write. And that's basically when the characters start stalking me.

— RENEA WINCHESTER

I always set out to write a novel I would enjoy reading.

— SARA JOHNSON

Writing is clearly a form of therapy.

— ANTHONY ABBOTT

If I can bring a story to the community that it represents, then that's what I want to do.

— ANNETTE SAUNOOKE CLAPSADDLE

When you write a novel, there's no certainty it's going to be published, there's no certainty anybody's going to read it. And when it became obvious to me it was gonna take quite a bit of time to do this, I spent about three days asking myself, do I really want to do this? And I thought, well, if one person reads it, if my son reads it one day, even when he's 40 years old, it'll be worth it.

— BOB DEANS

I will say that writing this book really ignited a love for writing books. I actually have another one that I'm already outlining. My boyfriend is like, can you just stop for a second?

— BONNE BARTRON

A writer has to have a devil-may-care attitude that is not sensitive to anybody's opinion or judgment, because there's every reason to believe, even if you have some areas of weakness, that what compels you and inspires you to pick up the pen in the first place can and should be trusted.

— CLAIRE FULLERTON

I've done several novels previously, but I wanted to write a book that was different.

— DALE NEAL

It just makes me happy. It's really an odd thing. I get inspiration from it. It's my passion. I like the way it makes me feel. And I like the way it makes other people feel when they read it. I like to make people laugh.

— DAVID OAKLEY

A lot of writers use their writing to work out things within their own life. I definitely subscribe to the Pat Conroy quote that writing is the only way that I was able to make sense of my own life.

— DORI ANN DUPRE

When I was thinking of doing it, I had lunch with a dear friend. I was feeling pretty down at the time. I said to her, there's a voice inside me saying, you have to write, you have to write. And I sometimes felt like if I don't write this book, I'll die. Now that sounds very dramatic. And it doesn't mean a physical death or that I would do anything to myself, but it was more like I was trying to understand.

— MIRINDA KOSSOFF

My main goal is that I want to entertain, I want people to enjoy reading a story because it's interesting, engaging. And that's partly because those are the stories that I grew up reading and enjoying when I was a kid. And I've always hated the idea that reading should be an 'eat your oatmeal' sort of experience. If it's not fun, thrilling, exciting, engaging, you've already failed as an author.

— PAOLO BACIGALUPI

I've always wanted to write, way back when I was in college. I had fantasies of writing things.

— OTHO ESKIN

I write because I love it so much. And it's a good escapism
for me. And therapy, you know, when life gets too
stressful.

— SUSAN MILLS WILSON

Prior to writing fiction, I was covering mass shootings,
executions, murders, anything that's really horrible in
Florida. So I really wanted to write a world that ended
happily, because so many times it doesn't in the real life.

— TARA LUSH

I always knew that I wanted to be a writer, but it's not
something you readily voice to people in the world. I
mean, who do you think you are, Hemingway? But I
always had this secret desire to write books.

— TRACY CLARK

If you want to do it because you've heard that writers get
rich and famous, you might want to rethink that. I can tell
you from personal experience that neither is guaranteed.

— FRYE GAILLARD

There's something powerful about writing it down. Whether that's the journal or the story, there's something in us that writing it down, getting it out that way, it does something for us, for our souls.

— Joani Elliott

I write because it's necessary. It's necessary for future generations that come after me. But I also write because it's necessary for my healing. If I didn't write in some genre, way, shape or form, I think I would crumble. I don't think that I would be able to be sane.

— Khalisa Rae

I didn't follow the usual path that people assume writers take of going to university and studying English and reading classics. I was in my mid 20s and my secretary job was made redundant, which means that my role is no longer required. The English expression for it sounds really depressing and sad. So I found myself on holiday with my boyfriend, who's now my husband, and all of his friends, and I found myself having this very drunken conversation with one of his friends at four o'clock in the morning about the fact that I no longer had a job and she said, what do you want to do when we get back to London, and I said, I'm going to sign up with some temping agencies and see if I can get another secretarial job. And she said, but surely there's something else you'd rather be doing. You could use this as an opportunity to change your life and do something that you've always wanted to do. I brought up that I always thought I'd write a novel one day, and she said, why don't you just do it, just write three chapters and if you do, I will take you out for dinner to your favorite restaurant. It was a bet. I wrote the three chapters, she took me to dinner at my favorite restaurant and those became the first three chapters of *House Party*, my first novel.

— LISA JEWELL

One day, I was thinking about where I came from, and where I'm at now. I decided to write the book, hoping it inspires people to say, okay, I'm in a tough environment, but this guy got out, he became successful, maybe I can, too.

— Marvin Williams

I'm writing now to try to figure out if I can write something in less than 25 years because I may not have that much time left.

— Michael Cody

People ask me, so what was your thought process in writing the novel? And I've said, I really didn't have any thought process, because I never intended to do it.

— Muriel Sheubrooks

I got the idea in my head that I could write a book and with my wife's prompting and encouragement, I set out to do it.

— Paul Attaway

I have a passion for it. I mean, my mind is a swirl of ideas and characters. And you don't have to be writing every day. Even if I'm not writing a word on a piece of paper or typing into a computer, my mind is working.

— ROBERT WALLACE

If you have that creativity thing, you should nurture it. Doesn't matter if you've got gray hair. It's never too late.

— STEVEN GROSSMAN

You always have to have a way to relax, you always have to have another way to think about things. And for me, it's writing history. That's always been my other thing.

— VANESSA RILEY

I think I write all the time. I think I've been writing all my life. And I mean, not sitting down consciously to put pen to paper or type. That's how my mind works.

— WALTER BENNETT

Art is the fuel for so much of a rich and fulfilling life.

— ALEX GEORGE

On my first date with my wife, I said I was gonna go to special forces, and I was gonna write a book. I was trying to get her clothes off. Years later, I came home one day and said, I think I'm gonna write a book, and my wife was like, whatever.

— BRAD TAYLOR

I got on this treadmill of writing, and I just love it. I can't not do it. I can't keep the stories that energize me from the page, no matter what happens with them.

— CHRIS FABRY

One of the reasons I got started writing was because I didn't read that well. I found that if I was observing what was happening in the classroom–like why all the cute girls like the horrible guys–and I would sit and write about that, my writing was clear.

— ERIC DEZENHALL

I had no idea what I was undertaking when I started this book at age 78. I suppose it was a three-year endeavor. If I had known it was going to take that long and that much work, I'm not sure I would have ever entered into the process. But I was gratified when it was done. It felt like a pretty decent effort.

— GENE HOOTS

I wanted to write it because my experience those three years in Africa in the Peace Corps was so enchanted.

— JACK ALLISON

My hope for the book is that it finds people who come to it, they can laugh, they can weep, but they can also leave it thinking about something they actually read. And I want that to move with them as they go forward into the day for however long it can.

— JASON MOTT

There's always some kind of personal aspect in a writing project. I mean, otherwise, I don't think I would feel compelled to be there.

— JILL MCCORKLE

I think this is true for most authors, you want people to be moved by your book, and to understand it.

— Katey Schultz

I approach my whole writing, whether I'm writing music, or whether writing nonfiction or fiction, as a desire to make the world better.

— Kathleen Basi

I talk to women's fiction authors and this is my favorite question, what was that spark of inspiration at the beginning that got you there?

— Lainey Cameron

My husband asked, what dreams are left unfulfilled for you? I said, I want to run a marathon and I want to write a novel. So on our first anniversary, we ran a marathon. And on our second anniversary, he said, where's your damn book?

— Pamela Fagan Hutchins

This neighbor came to me and said, I read your story, and tears started pouring down her cheeks. And she said, you got it right. And we stood there in the street for many minutes, both of us were in tears, and it was a huge shift for me to recognize that what I put on the page could reach out to other people. That experience moved me forward in believing that writing things, actually finishing them, and actually trying to put them out in the world, had value.

— REBECCA HODGE

I wrote it because there wasn't a resource, not one single book in the whole world up to this point, that told the whole story. Where did this thing come from? Why is it treated as legal?

— ROBERT FITZPATRICK

I write because–and you probably hear this on all these podcasts–I write because I can't not write.

— JANET SARJEANT

I like the arc that goes from injustice to justice. I turned to crime fiction because I wanted some kind of justice in the world.

— JANE ROSENTHAL

I certainly wanted to write an entertaining, compelling story, but as I got into the research about turn of the century politics, I realized that I needed to take a deeper dive into some of the more shameful personalities and events that characterized racial conditions, particularly in North Carolina and throughout the South, at the beginning of the 20th century.

— MICHAEL ALMOND

There's no way to predict whether your book will be published or read or appreciated. To me, that's really fundamental. If you enjoy the writing, you'll keep on doing it regardless.

— TERRY ROBERTS

I went on to live in some of the biggest cities all over the world, and I found that we've all got interesting stories to tell, we've all got so many things in common.

— GINA WILKINSON

I started writing and I got hooked completely early on. I realized I loved the process and I wanted to do it. And I started carving out time, which in reality meant giving up a whole bunch of stuff to be able to do it.

— KIMMERY MARTIN

What's so satisfying about writing is it's a way of communicating with other people.

— PETER GUZZARDI

What I love about being a poet is being able to take words to inspire people, to tell their story if they want their story told or to give perspective or be funny or be sad, and to give romance when that's needed. All those things are just another amazing part of being a poet.

— BLUZ

Poetry started for me in the fifth grade when I wrote a rap song for a school project. And then in sixth grade, I was introduced to Langston Hughes and the Harlem Renaissance and I just fell in love with the idea that you could infuse jazz cadences into the way you write.

— JAY WARD

I've been a writer since I was a little kid. Even before I could form actual letters, I practiced scribbling with a pencil on whatever scraps of paper I could find. It was like some part of me recognized my destined vocation long before I even knew what a writer was.

— KATHIE COLLINS

Writing poetry was a way for me to express all the things that I was experiencing. I've written since I was six years old. My first poem was actually about werewolves, believe it or not.

— SHANE MANIER

I use my writing as a way to really understand myself and what's going on around me. I really feel compelled. It's a way of telling the story to myself.

— PAM TURNER

I write because that's what I do best, better than anything else. I've always called myself a writer. Writing gives me a deeper insight into myself.

— SURABHI KAUSHIK

I used to write because I had to write in every job I ever had: grant writing, newsletters, press releases, promotional materials, etc. By the time I was in my 40s, I longed to have the time to write for myself.

— CHRIS ARVIDSON

Writing is a part of who I am – as simple as it sounds, I cannot imagine my life without putting words on the page. I have written in a journal since the days of diaries with little keys. Characters, plots and verses hang out together; writing it all down declutters my mind.

— CAROLINE KENNA

I only can know what I think when I see it down on
paper.

— CATHY PICKENS

Certainly there are more profitable lines of work than
being a novelist, but you know, I think all writers are
driven by this desire to communicate.

— GINA WILKINSON

As we all know, writing is a laborious process. We might as
well write what makes us happy and passionate, even if it
is the more defying route to go. So that is my challenge to
you: if you come to a fork in the writer's road, I hope you
choose to be assertive and write the book that takes you
out of your comfort zone and into a world of adventure.

— COLIN CERNIGLIA

I believe all writers write for the same reason, which has something to do with wanting to compare notes in this business of living. Whether we're published or by whom is not the point, the point is all writers are on the same path, propelled by an inexplicable urge to communicate, in whichever way they choose to tell a story.

— CLAIRE FULLERTON

Since being incarcerated, I have been diagnosed with a personality disorder, which was completely unknown to me and causes me to appear emotionless and detached. Yet, in my writing, I am able to express emotion effortlessly, allowing people to see a deeper, more intimate side of me that doesn't usually come through in everyday conversation.

— HEATHER WESTERFIELD

The reward for seeing your book in print makes all the hard work worthwhile.

— CARA BERTOIA

When I'm writing, I get lost in my characters' lives and can't wait to see how it turns out.

— JOE CONGEL

When other writers talked about getting blocked, I scoffed at them. My muse was strong. I never had a shortage of ideas. Nope, I had the opposite problem—too many of them. Then one day everything changed. I got stuck halfway through a manuscript with no idea how to fix it. After some serious soul searching, I remembered what I loved about writing. The escape.

— JILL BRASHEAR

Writing is a release, at least for me it always has been. I can speak my mind and pour raw, untapped emotions into stories. I can twist and mold the words however I want, to make it say what I want. To be able to make a scene come alive in a reader's mind is one of my most prized talents, as I'm sure it is for every author.

— SYDNEY HORNE

Stick with your ideal reader, who I discovered really is you. It is you who wants to get the information and you who wants to fill in all the gaps.

— AMY PEACOCK

Seeing how people respond, how it affects or inspires them to change their lives, has been a beautiful part of writing the book.

— BENJAMIN GILMER

I wish I had known how gratifying it is to write personal narratives. I never thought my own opinion was as valuable as the experts', the ones that are footnotes in my books. But now I see that my viewpoint has validity.

— RUTH LITTLE

I definitely am a believer that if you have the resources to do so to give away as many books as you can. Books are seeds. And if you wrote a book to add value to people, the only way it can add that value is if they read it.

— BECKY ROBINSON

I spent my early fiction writing career writing what I thought other people would expect from me, writing more literary, character-driven, quieter novels that I wasn't all that interested in. Then I asked myself, what do I most want to read? And the answer came back loud and clear. I want to write a ghost story. I love creepy stuff. I love creepy fiction. This is what I like to read. Why is this not what I'm writing? I wish I had told myself this when I was first starting out, but it's been a learning process.

— Jennifer McMahon

It was very difficult, gut wrenching, actually, to write about my divorce. I was writing to understand, to try to answer unanswerable questions, not that I came up with answers, but it was definitely very much worth doing. I feel a little lighter, perhaps.

— Cathia Friou

I thought it'd be fun to write a traditional thriller where the protagonist is in mortal peril in the first sentence and the roller coaster starts from there. It was a lot of fun to put together.

— Charlie Lovett

First thing, write what you want to write. If you like it,
that's the genre you should stick to because that's going to
come off the most authentic.

— SHERYL SMILEY-OLIPHANT

The writing process helped me flip the switch and see
things differently.

— KATHY IZARD

Once I realized there are novels out there where people
talk like I do and have a family like I do and do the things
that I do and eat the things that I do, that was the impetus
for me to get started.

— DONNA EVERHART

I knew at 11 years old that I wanted to be a writer.
Thanks, Nancy Drew.

— CATHY PICKENS

For me, writing is always about getting home. It's about getting to a place I want to be, a place I want to live in my imagination.

— ELAINE ORR

Please keep reading for the podcast founder's reflections on lessons he learned from the quotes in this book, but if you just can't wait to order the next book in the series, titled *Learning to Write*, you can at charlottereaderspodcast.com. Thank you for your support.

Learn more about Charlotte Readers Podcast and sign up for the podcast newsletter to get access to interesting content at charlottereaderspodcast.com.

REFLECTIONS -
LANDIS WADE

Lessons I Learned from the Quotes in this Book

One of the biggest lessons I learned from the quotes in this book is that no matter how much or how little money writers make (or lose) in their writing lives, or how demanding writing can be for them, they grab for their pens and fire up their computers mostly for the love of it. Writing is like a giant magnet that sucks them in. They have a common urge to create, to use letters, words, and sentences to tell stories, either about themselves, or others, or about characters they create and befriend in their writing chambers. They also write for therapy or to understand themselves or the world around them. They write for the sake of writing and they write for publication. They write to be remembered and they write to be heard and understood. And as more than one author said, they write because they can't not write.

Each writer quoted in this book combines their curious spirit with interesting life experiences, a combination that enriches what they write. As the late Anthony Abbott so eloquently said on the podcast, "Writing is not about writing, necessarily. Writing is about living. And the more deeply and fully you live, the more you are able to write."

There is hope in this book but there is also a lot of angst and humility. Case in point is the comment by John Hart, a *New York Times* bestselling author who is the only author ever to win the prestigious Edgar Award for consecutive novels. He said that the writing life is so unbelievably wonderful that he feels "deep down that the universe must have plans to take that all away." It makes him work even harder on his next book.

Similarly, bestselling UK author Lisa Jewell admits to making "so many mistakes" over the course of her career that it became part of the process, saying she "had to make mistakes over and over again to get to the point that I'm at now." Perhaps the key to good writing is not putting one word on the page after another but putting one bad word on the page after another–that is, making one mistake after another until it clicks.

As a former athlete, I see the writing life as a competition, but not the kind you may think. Claire Fullerton said "there is no competition out there" and Dori Ann Dupre said "I'm not in competition with anybody." They're right. It's why you see so many car dealers on the same busy road. Everyone needs a car, like everyone needs a book, so why not make it easy on them? So, no, authors are not so much in competition with each other. We're really in competition with ourselves. We are the hero in our own hero's writing journey, beset with obstacles, and bound to face reversals and setbacks. We have to fight hard for that happy ending to our journey.

And yet, sometimes, lightning can strike, as it did for Jason Mott, who won the National Book Award in 2022. He said he went "from literally answering the phones at Verizon Wireless to a year later having this book," describing his experience as very bizarre, "kind of the golden ticket syndrome where I got to go in Willy Wonka's chocolate factory."

What I love about reading the words in this book is that most authors are drinking the same Kool-Aid as me. I hear words like "the best of times" and "the worst of times" and I perk up. I've never been a long distance runner but I relate to the parallel that writing "is a marathon, not a sprint" and I laugh when they say "there is no finish line." I nod when I read that writing "shouldn't be painful," though it is at times, and that "it should be joyful," which it also is at times. I smile at the notion that writing "takes the right temperament," because patience is not my strong suit, and I marvel at how they get me when they use words like these to describe the writing life: fun; challenge; discovery; fulfilling; demanding; interesting; dream-like; hell; and best of all, "my happy place" where "I don't care about anything else in the world when I am writing."

These writers tell us to relax and enjoy the journey, to trust ourselves and write what we love, and to learn the rules, so we can break them. Huzzah to all that.

But most telling to me is the advice in these pages that it is never too late to start writing. I was a trial lawyer for most of my life, and while I loved to read for pleasure, I was too busy with work and life to get serious about writing. It wasn't until my mid-50s that I actually finished a story that turned into my first published novella. I was juiced by the process, coming home every night from work with a desire to write. My wife asked when I got home, "Where are you going?" I always said, "I'm going to find out what happens next."

A good book is full of conflict, something I was no stranger to in the practice of law. Becoming an author meant that I could do what I was never able to do before: control the conflict, and that is a wonderful place to be.

These writers say they have a desire to write and write well. They say creativity makes them feel alive. They say writing cleans them out. They say the part that surprises them is why they write. They say there are so many more ways to make money but they chose writing anyway. They say that a lot of writing is just bricklaying. They say that their characters are not wholly them, but there is always a piece of them in there as well. They say that writing is a release, that they get lost, that they escape, that they want to live in their imaginary worlds, and that writing is their most satisfactory way of communicating with other people. Amen and amen.

When compiling these quotes, I found the following words I voiced on the podcast about the writing life. I share them in the hope they will be helpful, and also, so I don't forget them.

- Most good ideas look crazy from the start. So embrace them and see what happens.
- I call myself a recovering trial lawyer because I work hard to get rid of old habits, to get beyond my past of trying to be practically perfect in every way—a trial lawyer's poison—and shift to being open in my 60s to creative ventures that might fail.
- I veered off for 35 years so I could earn a living before I started doing the things that you can't necessarily earn a living at.
- Though I hate to say it, because Julia Cameron might be listening, writing for the sake of writing can be its own routine. In addition to the peace

of mind that comes with writing, who knows what masterpieces it will produce.

- It is one thing to learn the mechanics of how to write a novel, and quite another to complete a novel. Writing a novel is hard work. It takes patience, endurance, discipline, and perseverance. There are plenty of opportunities to quit along the way. It is important to find ways not to quit.
- Asking questions is a fine way to connect to the writing process. You can ask questions about the craft of novel writing, but the better questions–the ones that will keep you writing your novel until "The End"–are the questions that stir your imagination.
- I believe you need to be a life-long learner, with both your writing career, and your marketing career. Ask questions. Read articles. Listen to podcasts. Talk about it.
- Writing can be a form of ad-libbing. You're into something, you're writing, and then something comes to you that you didn't expect.
- Be creative. Have fun with it.
- I have come to understand that writing a story begins with "what if."

Speaking of "what if," what if I had never taken up podcasting and asked the questions that led to this book? The answer is simple. I would have been poorer for it.

In the next book in this series, the topic is *Learning to Write*. You can support the podcast by ordering it now. Learn more about how at charlottereaderspodcast.com and sign up there for the podcast newsletter to get access to interesting readerly and writerly content.

Why Start a Podcast and Publish this Series?

As a trial lawyer for 35 years, I followed and wallowed in rules. And because I'd written three novellas in my mid-50s while practicing law and wanted to write a novel, I decided on the verge of retirement that I needed to learn more about the rules of writing, because frankly, you can't do a thing without rules.

To turn right on red, you need a rule. To hit a golf ball out of a hazard, you need a rule. To call back a touchdown, you need a rule. To cross a crowded uptown street, you need a rule, and you better follow it or you will get run over by a bus. I didn't want the writing bus to run over me so I started a podcast, something I knew nothing about how to do.

Did you hear the one about the lawyer who walked into a podcast studio? That was me, the punchline to my own joke. I knew how to interview witnesses. I figured: why not authors?

My quest began in the fall of 2018 with three things in mind. One, I would learn a new skill–how to podcast–and have fun doing it. Two, I would meet interesting authors, read their books, and help them promote their work. And three, I would ask authors about the secrets of writing.

I figured out pretty quickly that I was on to something, because except for the secrets writers hide in their novels until the very end, writers are the kind of people who are open to sharing their knowledge and experience. With few exceptions, the writing community is welcoming and supportive. How could it not be? The publishing world can be punishing.

I did not launch Charlotte Readers Podcast to publish a series about writing. If I had, I would have been more consistent with the questions I asked every author. But a funny thing happened on the way to and from the studio. The writers inspired and educated me with their stories and explanations of how they do what they do and it helped me publish my first full-length novel that has been well-reviewed and won more than five awards (something I say only because the novel would not have been what it is without the support of other writers). Thus, I decided, in gratitude for the writing guidance I received from our author guests, I would share what I learned, and what better way to do that than to let the authors speak for themselves?

If I were more practiced at lying, I'd say I learned the secrets–the VERY SECRETS to writing–and that those secrets, along with their first cousin–the VERY RULES of writing–are disclosed in this series. People are always looking for shortcuts, right?

What I discovered instead is that the rules and secrets of writing are like pieces in a gigantic jigsaw puzzle, where the writers are the puzzle pieces. Each writer has their own way of doing this thing called writing. And each writer has an interesting way of expressing their thoughts and feelings on a wide range of writing topics.

My father was inquisitive. "How much do they pay you to podcast?" I laughed. "They don't pay me, Dad." He shrugged. I could see the wheels turning. When your son reaches age 61 and loses his mind, it's time to let him learn from his mistakes.

Four years later, I have tried to learn from my mistakes, but the decision to podcast was not a mistake. The authors on the podcast have taught me, and while writing is mostly rewriting—a subject we cover in this series—I believe writing also is about learning and practicing.

Charlotte Readers Podcast began with the tagline: "where authors give voice to their written words." With this series, we've flipped the tagline to" "where authors give text to their spoken words."

Learn more about Charlotte Readers Podcast and sign up for the podcast newsletter to get access to interesting content at charlottereaderspodcast.com.

Acknowledgments

I am grateful to every writer whose honest, insightful, and helpful words appear in this series and to the listeners and listener supporters for tuning in and supporting the podcast.

I am grateful to Sarah Archer and Hannah Larrew for their participation as co-hosts on the Beyond 300 version of the podcast and their help and guidance with this project. Hannah is a dynamite publicist who reached out to me early and volunteered to help with podcast promotion because she loves reading and is a genuinely good person. Sarah is an excellent novelist and screenwriter and like Hannah, a good interviewer and conversationalist, but who (and Hannah will agree), has the best podcast voice of the three co-hosts. I have enjoyed our collaboration and the podcast is better for their involvement.

Also, thanks to Sarah Archer for the foreword to this book, Tim Barber at Dissect Designs for the covers, and Jennipher Tripp for the interior design.

Finally, thanks to my wife, Janet, who has put up with my many hours spent on my podcast and writing quests.

I hope you are as inspired by the written words in this series as I was when I first heard them. Learn more about Charlotte Readers Podcast and sign up for the podcast newsletter to get access to interesting readerly and writerly content at charlottereaderspodcast.com.

Write on!

About the Podcast Hosts

Landis Wade

Landis is the founder and a co-host of Charlotte Readers Podcast, where he has participated in more than 500 conversations with authors on books and writing.

He writes light-hearted legal thrillers and mysteries with a historical or holiday touch (cozies with a bit of a thrill).

He is a recovering trial lawyer turned podcaster and author (after 35 years of law practice) whose third book, *The Christmas Redemption*, won the Holiday category of the 12th Annual National Indie Excellence Awards, and whose recent novel, *Deadly Declarations*, was Winner in the 2022 American Fiction Awards in the Cozy Mystery category, a Finalist in the 2022 International Book Awards in the Thriller/Adventure Category, Bronze Medalist in the 2022 Readers' Favorite International Awards in the Legal Thriller category, and Finalist in both the Mystery/Suspense and Historical Categories of the 2022 Best Book Awards.

His short work has been published in *Writersdigest.com*, *The Charlotte Observer*, *Flying South*, and in various anthologies and he has won several contests, including the North

Carolina State Bar short story contest, and the Charlotte Writers' Club Ruth Moose Flash Fiction contest.

When he is not writing or podcasting, Landis enjoys reading, fly-fishing, golf, travel, playing with his grandchild, and spending time in the mountains and at the beach.

Learn more about his writing at his author website: landiswade.com.

Sarah Archer

Sarah appeared on Charlotte Readers Podcast as a guest author, then as a guest host, and then joined the podcast as a co-host with the Beyond 300 series beginning in June 2022.

Her debut novel, *The Plus One*, was published by Putnam in the US and received a starred review from Booklist. It has also been published in the UK, Germany, and Japan, and is currently in development for television.

As a screenwriter, she has developed material for MTV Entertainment, Snapchat, and Comedy Central. She is a Black List Screenwriting Lab fellow who has placed in competitions including the Motion Picture Academy's Nicholl Fellowship and the Tracking Board's Launch Pad.

Her short stories and poetry have been published in numerous literary magazines, and she has spoken and taught on writing to groups in several states and countries.

Learn more about her writing at her author website: saraharcherwrites.com.

Hannah Larrew

Hannah appeared on Charlotte Readers Podcast as a guest publicist, then as a guest host, and then joined the podcast as a co-host with the Beyond 300 series beginning in June 2022. She is a publicist and digital marketer for artists across the creative spectrum including award-winning authors, musicians, fine artists, and independent filmmakers. She has served as an editor, public relations specialist, and marketer for both editorial firms and media outlets, including Pulitzer Prize winning newspaper, *The Post & Courier*.

After working first-hand in several different facets of the publishing and media industries, Hannah brought her experience to launch her own boutique marketing and public relations firm, Spellbound PR. Spellbound takes traditional PR tactics and puts a modern digital spin on storytelling campaigns to identify and reach target markets. Hannah has always been an avid reader and writer and contributor to several digital publications. She currently splits her time between Cincinnati, Ohio, and Charleston, South Carolina, with her husband, daughter, and two Goldendoodles.

Learn more about her at her website: spellboundpublicrelations.com

Writer Index

Below is a list of every author featured in the eight books in *The Write Quotes* series and the books in which they are quoted.

The fact that some authors are quoted in fewer books than others has nothing to do with their scope of knowledge or experience and more to do with the focus of their particular episodes (whether, for example, the focus was more on their books than on craft questions, or whether the craft questions asked were directed to a particular topic rather than a variety of topics), and whether other authors appeared in more episodes than them. When authors spoke primarily to one craft topic, they may appear in fewer books but are likely to be quoted more times than others in a particular book that deals with that topic. If their names appear more than once in the list, it is because they appeared on the podcast more than once.

You can find the entire Alphabetical Guest List, the Guest List By Region, the Community Blog, and the Community Vlog at charlottereaderspodcast.com. You can also sign up there for the podcast newsletter to get access to interesting readerly and writerly content.

And if you would like access to more than 150 exclusive episodes on our Patreon channel where many of these authors discuss a variety of writing topics, check out: patreon.com/charlottereaderspodcast.

Aaron Gwyn = Books 1, 2, 3, 4, 5
Abigail DeWitt = Books 1, 2, 3, 4, 5, 6
A.J. Hartley = Books 1, 2, 3, 4, 5, 6, 7, 8
Akbar Hussain = Books 2, 3
Alex George = Books 1, 2, 3, 4, 5, 6
Alice Osborn = Books 5, 6, 8
Alison Paul Klakowicz = Books 1, 2, 8
Allie Coker = Books 1, 2, 3, 5, 6, 7
Allison Hutchcraft = Books 2, 4, 5, 7
Amber Smith (1) = Books 1, 2, 3, 4, 5, 6, 7, 8
Amber Smith (2) = Books 1, 2, 3, 4, 5, 6, 7, 8
Amy Peacock = Books 1, 4, 6, 8
Amy Rogers = Books 3, 4, 5
Amy Williams = Books 1, 2, 3, 6, 7
Amy Willoughby-Burle = Books 1, 2, 3, 4, 5, 6, 7, 8
Anissa Gray = Books 1, 2, 3, 4
Ann Campanella = Books 3, 4, 5, 6, 7, 8
Anna Jean Mayhew = Books 4, 6
Annette Saunooke Clapsaddle = Books 1, 2, 3, 4, 5, 6, 7, 8
Anthony Abbott = Books 1, 4, 5
Arshia Simkin = Books 2, 6
Augustus White = Book 7
Avery Caswell = Books 3, 4, 5, 7
Barbara Johnson = Books 1, 2, 3, 6
Barry Swanson = Books 1, 2, 3, 4, 5, 6, 7

Becky Robinson = Books 1, 4, 5, 7, 8
Belle Boggs = Books 1, 2
Belinda Smith-Sullivan = Books 4, 5
Benjamin Gilmer = Books 1, 3, 4, 5, 7
Bess Kercher = Books 1, 2, 4, 6, 7
Bethany Johnson = Book 3
Betsy Mack = Books 1, 3, 7
Bluz = Books 1, 5
Bob Deans = Books 1, 4, 5
Bobby Finger = Books 1, 2, 3, 4, 5, 7, 8
Bobby Nash = Books 1, 2, 3, 4, 5, 6, 8
Bonne Bartron = Books 1, 3, 4, 7, 8
Brad Taylor = Books 1, 2, 3, 4, 5, 6, 7, 8
Brett Marie = Books 1, 2, 6, 7
Brian Andrews = Books 2, 3, 4, 6
Brian Baltosiewich = Books 2, 3, 4
Brian Langhoff = Book 6
Brooke Reynolds = Books 2, 3, 8
Bruce Holsinger = Books 3, 4, 8
Bryan Mitchell = Book 3
Bryn Chancellor = Books 3, 6, 8
Bud Schill = Books 1, 2, 3, 4
Caleb Johnson = Books 1, 2, 3, 4, 7
Camille Martin = Books 1, 5, 7
Cara Bertoia = Books 1, 2, 6
Carey Henry Keefe = Books 2, 7
Caroline Kenna = Books 1, 2, 5, 6, 7
Carolyn Baker = Books 1, 3, 4, 5, 6, 7, 8
Carrie Knowles (1) = Books 1, 2, 3, 4, 5, 6, 7, 8
Carrie Knowles (2) = Books 1, 2, 3, 4, 5, 6, 7, 8
Casey Eanes = Books 2, 3, 4, 5, 6
Cat Warren = Books 1, 2, 5, 6
Cathey Daniels = Books 2, 3, 4

Cathia Friou = Books 1, 5

Catherine Goodman Farley = Books 3, 4, 6, 7, 8

Cathy Pickens (1) = Books 1, 2, 3, 4, 5, 6, 7, 8

Cathy Pickens (2) = Books 1, 2, 3, 4, 5, 6, 7, 8

Cathy Pickens (3) = Books 1, 2, 3, 4, 5, 6, 7, 8

Charles Edwards = Books 3, 7

Charles Fiore = Books 1, 3, 4, 5, 6, 8

Charles Israel = Books 1, 2, 4, 6, 7

Charles Oldham = Books 2, 3, 8

Charlie Lovett (1) = Books 1, 2, 3, 4, 5, 6, 7, 8

Charlie Lovett (2) = Books 1, 2, 3, 4, 5, 6, 7, 8

Chris Arvidson = Books 1, 2, 3, 5, 6, 7, 8

Charlotte Dune = Book 8

Chris Fabry = Books 1, 2, 3, 4, 5, 6, 7

Christopher Davis = Books 2, 3, 4, 5, 7

Christopher Singleton = Books 2, 4, 5, 6, 8

Christy Hallberg (1) = Books 1, 3, 4, 5, 6, 7

Christy Hallberg (2) = Books 1, 3, 4, 5, 6, 7

C.J. Box = Books 1, 2, 4, 5, 7

Claire Fullerton = Books 1, 3, 4, 5, 6, 7, 8

Cliff Yeargin = Books 1, 2, 3, 4, 5, 7

Clyde Edgerton = Books 1, 2, 3, 4, 5, 6, 7

Colin Cerniglia = Book 1

Cortney Donelson = Books 3, 5

Craig Johnson = Books 1, 2, 3, 4, 5, 6, 7

Craig Nova = Books 1, 2, 3, 4, 7

Culley Holderfield = Books 1, 2, 3, 5, 7

Cynthia Newberry Martin = Books 4, 5, 7, 8

Dale Neal = Books 1, 2, 3, 4, 5, 6, 7

Danielle Stewart (1) = Books 1, 2, 6, 7, 8

Danielle Stewart (2) = Books 1, 2, 6, 7, 8

Danny Bernstein = Books 2, 4, 5, 6, 8

Dannye Romine Powell = Books 1, 2, 3, 5, 7

David Baldacci (1) = Books 1, 2, 3, 4, 5, 6, 7, 8
David Baldacci (2) = Books 1, 2, 3, 4, 5, 6, 7, 8
David Collins = Books 4, 5
David Joy = Books 1, 2, 3, 4
David Oakley = Books 1, 5, 7, 8
David Poston = Books 1, 2, 4, 5
David Radavich = Books 1, 2, 3, 4, 6
David Rudolf = Book 1
Dawn Hardy = Books 6, 8
Dede Wilson = Books 2, 3, 4
Delphine McClelland = Books 3, 7
Dennis Carrigan = Books 2, 5
Diane C. McPhail = Book 4
Dixie Gamble = Books 2, 3, 4, 6, 8
Donna Love Wallace = Books 1, 2, 3
Donna Everhart = Books 1, 3, 4, 5, 6
Dori Ann Dupre = Books 1, 6, 7, 8
D.S. Davis = Books 1, 6, 7
Ed Southern = Books 1, 2, 3, 4, 5, 6, 7
Edward Di Gangi = Books 1, 3, 4, 6, 7
Elaine Kelly = Book 6
Elaine Orr = Books 1, 2, 3, 4, 5, 6
Elan Barnehama = Books 2, 3, 4, 6, 7, 8
Eliot Parker = Books 2, 3, 5, 6, 7, 8
Elizabeth Holmes = Books 2, 4
Ellen Butler = Books 1, 2, 3, 4, 5, 7, 8
Ellen Morris = Books 1, 2, 3, 4, 5, 7, 8
Ellyn Ritterskamp = Books 2, 6, 7, 8
Emily Cataneo = Books 1, 2, 3, 4, 5, 6
Emily Johnson = Books 4, 6, 8
Emme Lund = Books 1, 2, 3, 4, 6, 7
Eric Dezenhall = Books 1, 2, 3, 5, 6
Erika Hoffman = Book 5

Fabi Preslar = Books 1, 7

Frank Morelli = Books 1, 2, 3, 4, 5, 6, 7, 8

Frye Gaillard = Books 1, 2, 3, 4, 5

Gail Martin = Books 1, 2, 3, 4, 6, 8

Gail Peck = Books 2, 6, 7, 8

Gary Edgington = Books 2, 3, 5, 6, 7

Gary Powell = Books 4, 5

Gavin Edwards = Books 2, 3, 4, 5, 7

Gene Hoots = Books 1, 3, 4, 6, 7, 8

George Arnold = Books 1, 2, 3, 4, 5

George Hovis (1) = Books 1, 2, 3, 4, 5, 6

George Hovis (2) = Books 1, 2, 3, 4, 5, 6

George Trudeau = Book 2

Gilda Syverson = Books 1, 2, 3, 4, 5, 6

Gina Wilkinson = Books 1, 2, 3, 4, 5

Grace Ocasio = Books 2, 3, 4, 5, 6

Grace Sammon = Books 2, 3, 5, 6, 8

Greg Jarrell = Book 4

Halli Gomez = Books 2, 3, 4, 5, 6, 7

Hannah Larrew = Books 6, 8

Hans Watford = Books 2, 3, 4, 5, 7

Heather Bell Adams = Books 1, 2, 3, 4, 6, 7

Heather Newton = Books 1, 2, 3, 4, 5, 6, 7, 8

Heather Westerfield = Book 1

Heidi Brown = Books 1, 2, 3, 4, 6, 8

Holly Hughes = Books 1, 2, 3, 5, 6, 7, 8

Howard Covington, Jr = Books 1, 2, 3, 4, 5, 6

Hope Anderson = Books 1, 2, 3, 4, 5, 7, 8

Ian Malone = Books 1, 2, 3, 5, 6

Irene Blair Honeycutt = Books 1, 2, 4, 5, 6, 7

J.A. Walsh = Books 1, 2, 3, 4, 5, 6, 7

J.D. DuPuy = Books 1, 3, 4, 6

Jack Allison = Books 1, 2, 3, 5, 7

Jack Grossman = Books 4, 5
Jacqui Castle = Books 1, 2, 3, 6, 7, 8
Jade Dee = Books 1, 2, 6, 7, 8
Jaki Shelton Green = Books 1, 2, 3, 4, 5, 6, 7
Jan Notzon = Books 3, 4, 5, 8
Jane Rosenthal = Books 1, 2, 3, 4, 5, 7
Janet Sarjeant = Books 1, 2, 3, 4, 7
Jason Mott = Books 1, 2, 4, 5, 7, 8
Jay Ward = Books 1, 2, 5
Jean Grant = Book 8
Jeanne Adams = Books 1, 3, 6, 8
Jeff Jackson = Books 1, 3, 4, 5, 6, 8
Jeffrey Wilson = Books 1, 5
Jenifer Ruff (1) = Books 1, 3, 5, 6, 7, 8
Jenifer Ruff (2) = Books 1, 3, 5, 6, 7, 8
Jennie Liu = Books 6, 8
Jennifer Dasal = Books 1, 3, 4, 8
Jennipher Tripp = Books 2, 8
Jennifer McMahon = Books 1, 3, 4, 5
Jerry McGee = Book 3
Jessica Peterson = Books 1, 3, 5, 7, 8
Jill Brashear = Book 1
Jill McCorkle = Books 1, 2, 3, 4, 5, 6, 7
Jim Hamilton = Books 2, 4
Jim Mitchem = Book 2
Joani Elliott = Books 1, 2, 3, 5, 6, 7, 8
Jodi Helmer = Books 1, 5, 6, 7, 8
Joe Congel = Books 1, 2, 7
Joel Burcat = Books 1, 2, 3, 4, 5, 6, 7, 8
Joel Shulkin = Book 4
John Gerdy (1) = Books 1, 2, 4
John Gerdy (2) = Books 1, 2, 4
John Gilstrap = Books 1, 2, 3, 4, 5, 6, 7, 8

John Hart = Books 1, 2, 3, 4, 5, 7, 8
John Hood = Books 2, 3, 5, 8
John Russell = Books 1, 3, 4
Johnnie Bernhard = Books 2, 7
Jon Bassoff = Books 1, 2, 3, 4, 5, 7
Jon Buchan = Books 1, 2, 3, 4, 5, 7
Jon Sealy = Books 1, 3
Jonathan Lerner = Book 4
Jordan O'Donnell = Books 1, 4
Jordan Wade = Books 3, 7
Joseph Bathanti = Book 5
Joseph Mills = Books 1, 2, 3, 4, 5, 6
Joy Callaway = Books 1, 2, 3, 4, 8
Judith Schindler = Book 3
Judy Goldman (1) = Books 1, 2, 3, 4, 5, 6, 7
Judy Goldman (2) = Books 1, 2, 3, 4, 5, 6, 7
Judy Goldman (3) = Books 1, 2, 3, 4, 5, 6, 7
Judy Seldin-Cohen = Books 3, 5, 6, 8
Julia Jordan-Zachery = Books 1, 2, 3, 4, 6, 7
Justin Hunt = Books 2, 3, 4, 5
Kaitlyn Jain = Books 3, 4, 5, 7
Kamaria Delaney = Books 1, 3, 4, 5
Karen McElmurray = Books 1, 2, 5
Karla FC Holloway = Book 4
Katey Schultz = Books 1, 2, 3, 4, 5, 6, 7
Katherine Snow Smith = Books 1, 3
Kathie Collins (1) = Books 1, 2, 4, 5, 6
Kathie Collins (2) = Books 1, 2, 4, 5, 6
Kathleen Basi = Books 1, 3, 4, 5, 6
Kathleen Burkinshaw = Books 1, 5, 6
Kathryn Schwille = Books 1, 2, 3, 4
Kathy Izard = Books 1, 2, 3, 4, 5, 6, 7, 8
Kelly Finley = Book 8

Ken Chamlee = Book 5
Kevin McIlvoy = Books 1, 2, 3, 4, 5, 6, 7
Kevin Winchester = Books 2, 3, 4, 5, 6, 7
Khalisa Rae = Books 1, 2, 4, 5, 6, 7, 8
Kia Flow = Books 4, 5
Kim Wright = Books 1, 2, 3, 4, 5, 6, 7
Kimberley Motley = Books 3, 5
Kimmery Martin = Books 1, 2, 3, 4, 5, 6, 7, 8
Kristen Rademacher = Books 3, 4, 5, 7, 8
Kristy Harvey = Books 1, 2, 3, 5, 6, 7, 8
Larry Farber = Books 1, 3
Lainey Cameron = Books 1, 2, 3, 4, 5, 6, 7, 8
Lainey Cameron = Books 1, 2, 3, 4, 5, 6, 7, 8
Landis Wade (1) = Books 1, 2, 3, 4, 5, 6, 7, 8
Landis Wade (2) = Books 1, 2, 3, 4, 5, 6, 7, 8
Landis Wade (3) = Books 1, 2, 3, 4, 5, 6, 7, 8
Laura King Edwards = Books 1, 3, 5
Lauren Jacobs = Books 4, 7
Laurie Smithwick = Book 4
Lee Matalone = Books 1, 2, 3, 4, 5, 6, 7, 8
Lee Zacharias = Book 7
Leighton Ford = Book 2
Leslie Hooton (1) = Books 5, 6, 7
Leslie Hooton (2) = Books 5, 6, 7
Lexi Aidyn = Books 1, 2, 7
Linda Phillips = Books 3, 4, 5, 8
Lisa Jewell = Books 1, 2, 3, 4, 5, 6, 7, 8
Lisa Williams Kline = Books 2, 3, 4, 5, 6
Lisa Saunders = Books 2, 3, 4, 5, 7
Lori Epting = Books 2, 3, 4, 5, 6, 7, 8
Lucy McLaren = Books 1, 7, 8
Lynda Bouchard = Books 6, 7, 8
M.L. Huie = Books 3, 4, 7, 8

M. William Phelps = Books 1, 2, 3, 4, 5, 7
Maggie Smith = Books 1, 2, 3, 4, 6, 8
Malika Stevely = Books 4, 5
Marc Jampole = Books 3, 4, 5, 6, 7, 8
Marianne Sprangers = Books 3, 7
Mark de Castrique (1) = Books 1, 3, 4, 5, 6
Mark de Castrique (2) = Books 1, 3, 4, 5, 6
Mark de Castrique (3) = Books 1, 3, 4, 5, 6
Mark Peres = Books 3, 4, 7, 8
Mark West (1) = Books 1, 2, 4, 5, 6, 7, 8
Mark West (2) = Books 1, 2, 4, 5, 6, 7, 8
Martha Kearse = Books 2, 4
Martin Clark = Books 1, 3, 4, 7, 8
Martin Mongiello Books 3, 8
Martin Settle = Books 1, 2, 3, 4, 5, 7
Marvin Williams = Books 1, 7
Mary Ann Claud = Books 1, 4, 5
Mary Bess Dunn = Books 1, 2, 5, 7
Mary Flinn = Books 5, 6, 8
Mary Kratt = Books 2, 4, 5
Mary Laura Philpott = Books 1, 2, 4, 5
Mary Salisbury = Books 2, 7
Mary Tribble = Books 1, 2, 3, 4, 5, 6, 7, 8
Marybeth Whalen = Books 1, 2, 3, 4, 5, 7, 8
Matt Doherty = Book 7
Matthew Duffus = Books 2, 3, 4, 5, 6, 8
Maureen Miller = Books 2, 3, 4, 8
Maureen Ryan Griffin = Books 1, 2, 3, 4, 6, 7, 8
Maureen Sherbondy = Books 1, 2, 3, 4, 5
Meagan Lucas = Books 1, 2, 4, 5, 7
Megan Miranda (1) = Books 1, 2, 4, 5, 6
Megan Miranda (2) = Book 1, 2, 4, 5, 6
Meredith Ritchie = Books 2, 3, 4, 5, 6, 7

Michael Almond = Books 1, 2, 3, 4, 5, 8

Michael Cody = Books 1, 2, 3, 4, 5, 7

Michael Croley = Books 1, 2, 5, 7, 8

Michael Polelle = Books 1, 2, 3, 4, 5, 6, 7

Michele Tracy Berger = Books 1, 2, 3, 4, 5, 6, 7

Micki Morency = Book 2

Mike Bond = Books 1, 2, 3, 4, 5, 7

Mimi Herman = Books 3, 4, 5

Mirinda Kossoff = Books 1, 2, 3, 4, 6, 7

Miriam Herin = Books 2, 3, 4, 6, 7

Misha Lazzara = Books 1, 2, 3, 4, 5, 6, 7

Molly Barker = Book 5

Molly Grantham = Books 1, 3, 5, 7

Muriel Sheubrooks = Books 1, 2, 3, 6, 7, 8

Nancy Northcott = Books 2, 5, 6, 8

Nancy Stancill = Books 1, 2, 3, 4, 5

Natasha Boyd = Books 3, 4, 5, 7

Natasha Tynes = Books 1, 2, 3, 4, 5, 7

Neil Carmichael = Books 3, 6, 8

Nicholas Graham = Books 3, 4, 5

Nicole Ayers = Books 1, 2, 3, 4, 5, 6, 7

Nora Gaskin = Books 1, 2, 3, 4, 5, 6, 8

Otho Eskin = Books 1, 2, 4, 5, 6

Paloma Capanna = Books 1, 3, 4

Pamela Fagan Hutchins = Books 1, 2, 3, 4, 5, 6, 7, 8

Paolo Bacigalupi = Books 1, 2, 3, 4, 5, 6, 7

Pam Kelley = Books 2, 3, 4, 6

Pam Turner = Books 1, 5

Patrice Gopo = Books 1, 2, 3, 4, 5, 6

Patti Meredith = Books 2, 3, 6

Paul Attaway (1) = Books 1, 2, 3, 4, 5, 6, 7, 8

Paul Attaway (2) = Books 1, 2, 3, 4, 5, 6, 7, 8

Paul Kurzeja = Books 2, 4

Paul Lamb = Books 3, 5
Paul Reali = Books 1, 2, 3, 4, 5, 6, 7
Paula Martinac = Books 1, 3, 4, 5, 7
Paulette Stout = Book 8
Peter Guzzardi = Books 1, 2, 3, 5, 6, 7, 8
Peter Reinhart = Books 1, 2, 3, 4, 5, 6, 7
Philip Gerard = Books 2, 3, 4, 5, 7
Phillip Lewis = Books 1, 2, 3, 4, 6, 7, 8
Rachael Brooks = Books 1, 5, 7
Randell Jones = Books 1, 2, 3, 4, 5, 6
Rebecca Hodge = Books 1, 2, 3, 4, 5, 6, 8
Rebecca McClanahan = Books 4, 5, 7
Reita Pendry = Books 1, 2, 6, 7
Renea Winchester = Books 1, 2, 3, 4, 5
Rick Bleiweiss = Books 1, 3, 4, 5, 6
Rick Pryll = Books 1, 2, 3, 4, 5, 7, 8
Rita Woods = Books 1, 3, 4, 7
Robert Conrad = Books 1, 2, 3
Robert Fitzpatrick = Books 1, 4, 5, 7, 8
Robert Gwaltney = Books 1, 2, 3, 4, 5, 7, 8
Robert Inman = Books 1, 2, 3, 4, 5, 7
Robert Wallace = Books 1, 2, 3, 4, 5, 6, 7
Robert Whitlow = Books 1, 2, 3, 4, 5, 6, 8
Roger Colberg = Books 2, 3, 4, 6, 7
Roland Beckerman = Books 1, 3, 7
Ron Rash = Books 1, 2, 4, 5, 6, 7
Rose Senehi = Books 1, 3, 4, 6, 8
Rosie Molinary = Books 1, 2, 4, 7
Rosy Crumpton = Books 1, 3, 4
Rue Sparks = Book 8
Ruth Little = Books 1, 2, 6
Ryan McGee = Book 5
Sam McGee (1) = Books 1, 2, 3, 4, 7

Sam McGee (2) = Books 1, 2, 3, 4, 7
Sandra L. Young = Books 2, 4, 5, 6, 7, 8
Sandy Hill = Books 1, 2, 4, 5
Sara Johnson = Books 1, 2, 3, 4, 5, 6
Sarah Archer = Books 1, 2, 3, 4, 5, 6, 7, 8
Scott Fowler = Books 1, 2, 3, 4, 5, 7
Scott Gates = Books 2, 3, 4
Scott Huler = Books 1, 2, 3, 4, 7
Scott Syfert = Book 4
Seth Ervin = Books 1, 2, 3, 4, 5, 6, 7
Shane Manier = Books 1, 5
Sharon Dukett = Book 8
Sheila Myers = Books 2, 4, 5, 7
Sheryl Smiley-Oliphant = Books 1, 4, 7, 8
Sonya Ramsey = Book 4
Sita Romero = Book 6
Sophia Henry = Books 1, 5, 8
Sophie Cousens = Books 1, 2, 3, 4, 5, 7
Stacey Simms = Books 1, 5
Stacy Hawks = Books 1, 3, 4, 6, 7, 8
Stephen Eoannou = Books 2, 4, 5, 6, 7
Steve Berry = Books 1, 2, 3, 4, 5, 6, 7
Steven Grossman = Books 1, 2, 3, 4, 5, 6, 7, 8
Surabhi Kaushik = Books 1, 6, 7
Susan Proctor = Books 1, 3, 4
Susan Mills Wilson = Books 1, 2, 3, 4, 5, 6, 8
Susan Zurenda = Books 1, 2, 3, 4, 5
Susannah Marren = Books 2, 3, 4, 6, 7, 8
Suzanne Goodwyn = Book 8
Sydney Horne = Books 1, 2, 4
Tammy Euliano = Books 2, 3, 4, 5, 6, 7, 8
Tammy Harrow = Book 5
Tamra Wilson = Books 1, 2, 6, 8

Tara Lush = Books 1, 3, 4, 5, 8

Terra Kelly = Books 1, 2, 5

Terry Roberts (1) = Books 1, 3, 4, 5, 7

Terry Roberts (2) = Books 1, 3, 4, 5, 7

Tessa Afshar = Book 3

Therese Anne Fowler = Books 1, 2, 3, 5, 6

Tim Eichenbrenner = Books 3, 6, 7, 8

Tim Reinhardt = Books 3, 4, 5, 6, 7

Tom Hanchett = Books 1, 2, 3, 5

Tom Stewart = Books 2, 3

Tommy Tomlinson = Books 3, 5, 6, 7

Tracey Buchanan = Book 7

Tracie Barton-Barrett = Books 1, 3, 5, 6, 7, 8

Tracy Clark = Books 1, 2, 3, 4, 5, 6, 7

Tracy Curtis (1) = Books 1, 2, 3, 4, 5, 6

Tracy Curtis (2) = Books 1, 2, 3, 4, 5, 6

Valerie Nieman = Books 2, 3, 5, 6, 7

Vanessa Riley = Books 1, 3, 4, 5, 7, 8

Vernon Glenn = Books 1, 2, 3, 8

Wade Rouse = Books 1, 3, 4, 5

Walter Bennett = Books 1, 2, 4, 5, 7

Webb Hubbell = Books 1, 2, 3, 5

Wade Foley = Book 8

Wiley Cash = Books 1, 2, 3, 4, 5, 6, 7, 8

Wilnona Marie = Books 1, 3, 7, 8